Alleluia is the Song of the Desert

C owley Publications is a ministry of the brothers of the Society of Saint John the Evangelist, a monastic order in the Episcopal Church. Our mission is to provide books and resources for those seeking spiritual and theological formation. Cowley Publications is committed to developing a new generation of writers and teachers who will encourage people to think and pray in new ways about spirituality, reconciliation, and the future.

Alleluia is the Song of the Desert

An Exercise for Lent and Other Sacred Times

Lawrence D. Hart

Cowley Publications
Cambridge, Massachusetts

Published in the United States of America by Cowley Publications, a division of the Society of Saint John the Evangelist. No portion of this book may be reproduced, stored in or introduced into a retrieval system, or transmitted, in any form or by any means-including photocopying-without the prior written permission of Cowley Publications, except in the case of brief quotations embedded in critical articles and reviews.

Library of Congress Cataloging-in-Publication Data:
Hart, Lawrence D.
    Alleluia is the song of the desert : an exercise for Lent and other sacred times / Lawrence D. Hart.
    p. cm.
Includes bibliographical references.
    ISBN 1-56101-250-5 (pbk.)
    1. Jesus Christ--Temptation--Meditations. 2. Jesus Christ—Crucifixion—Meditations. 3. Jesus Christ—Appearances—Meditations. 4. Lent—Prayer-books and devotions--English. I. Title.
BT355.H35 2003
242'.34--dc22
                                2003023879

Cover design: Gary Ragaglia

This book was printed in Canada on acid-free paper.

Cowley Publications
907 Massachusetts Avenue
Cambridge, Massachusetts 02139
800-225-1534 • www.cowley.org

*This book is dedicated in loving gratitude
to my mother, Jewell Hart,
who taught me to read and to think,
to aspire to compassion and integrity,
and to find my consolation in Christ.*

Contents

Foreword

Lawrence Hart has produced a work that can well hold its place in the great apophatic tradition of meditations designed to call us into an ever deeper relationship with God. Here scripture and other ancient spiritual traditions are seamlessly woven together with contemporary intellectual and scientific theory into a unity that lures the reader into the very heart of that unity.

Hart's primary focus is upon the necessity of emptying ourselves in order to be filled. The path to this openness is spiritual discipline, lived into through a lifetime a day at a time. Yet throughout the work, Hart does the interesting work of making words and images that commonly have negative connotations into positives—boredom as a path to finding meaning, self-surrender as gain, being driven into the desert as a way to prepare us for some work of love. These and other terms, such as sin, lack, loss, testing, and giving up, are all imbued with a kind of shining glory that entices the reader further in.

The first part of the book consists of seven biblically-based meditations on some of the chaotic events of Jesus' life—first, his temptations in the desert for the forty days after his baptism, and then his death and resurrection. The focus of all is the kind of ministry to which Jesus was called, and in turn the kind of life to which we are called as followers of Jesus. This is no simple "how-to" book, but rather a profound challenge to consider a totally different kind of life. He approaches these life changes from several different angles—each leading to the deep kind of knowing that is God's gift to the true seeker.

Also of great value is the emphasis on and aid for small group work, which makes up the last part of the book. Nearly fifty years ago, the pastoral theology professor at our seminary noted that "something" happens in the small group that doesn't happen anywhere else. "We don't quite know what it is, but we know it's good." Hart's comparison is illuminating in this regard, as he compares such small group work to a monastic desert community where all can grow toward a deeper experience of God's presence. Thus the book, which is valuable for an individual, is further enhanced by the "something" made possible by the creation of the seeking community. It is truly a winsome invitation to a journey in common pilgrimage.

Hart also supplies detailed weekly outlines for group meetings, so that even the most inexperienced facilitator can lead a group. His suggestions for prayers, reflections, formats, even settings, are down-to-earth and easily translated into action. Here profound explorations are presented in clear, available language.

Lawrence Hart has given us an invitation to go through the worst despair the world can present into a shared Alleluia to a living Christ. Come, he urges us, join the journey into the cosmic dimensions of the glory of the Christ, who being lifted up, draws all things to himself. And so join the Alleluia.

Jean Dalby Clift
Canon Pastor Emeritus
Diocese of Colorado

Acknowledgements

I thank, first of all, my wife, Brenda, for her part in this effort. She has played a significant role in everything worthwhile I have done in my life and has been a major influence in my spiritual formation. Without the encouragement of the Rev. Dr. Wallace Clift, Canon Theologian of the Diocese of Colorado, I would not have submitted this book for publication. I thank the Rev. Michelle Danson for reading the manuscript, and Cheryl Fleharty for providing such generous technical computer support. I am grateful for the editorial assistance of Ulrike Guthrie in smoothing out some of the rough spots; and, of course, I am appreciative of Kevin Hackett, all those at Cowley Publications, and the Society of Saint John the Evangelist for bringing this modest work to fruition. Finally, my thanks to the people of Saint George in the Glen for their support, love, and patience while I researched and wrote this book.

Introduction

For thousands of years deserts have been geographical centers of spiritual formation and direct encounter with God. In traditional Christian spirituality, men and women seeking the kind of purification that leads to wisdom of heart, to "a further union, a deeper communion," have sought out the desert places. But the physical desert is not my primary concern. What I am most interested in here is the desert as a state of mind or consciousness, a spiritual practice, an inner place where we come to have a first-hand experience of God.

The practices of Lent are meant to lead us to this interior desert. The forty days of Lent are a time of *metanoia* (repentance), of emptying our hearts so that they can be filled with that love and presence of Christ which we celebrate at Easter. Entering Lent, then, can be imagined as entering the silence of a vast and empty desert.

Although these meditations were written with the Lenten season in mind, there is no reason why they cannot be used at other times as well. My only suggestion is that you might want to stay with the forty-day format. The number forty occurs frequently in the Old Testament and the New. In the Old, the rain that caused the flood in the time of Noah lasts forty days. The journey of the Jewish people through the desert to the Promised Land lasts forty years. Elijah walks forty days to the holy wilderness mountain of Horeb, where he encounters God in mystical silence. In the New Testament, Jesus spends forty days praying and fasting in a desert place. And so, even if you are using these meditations at a time other than Lent, you may find it beneficial to retain the symbolism of forty days of prayer.

You can certainly read or use this book as an individual; however, it is written primarily with small spiritual formation groups in mind. I have divided it into seven chapters with the idea that by reading one chapter each week, beginning with the week of Ash Wednesday and ending with Easter Week, it will take a group through Lent and Easter. There are questions in the text of each chapter that can be discussed in a group setting, or on which you can reflect alone as you are reading. A set of fairly detailed exercises for small groups has been included in Appendix C.

In order to enhance ease of reading, and because this is a set of meditations rather than an academic exploration of desert spirituality, there are no footnotes. However, references for quoted works and Scripture citations in each chapter may be found in the endnotes at the back of the book.

I have drawn on the translations of *The Contemporary English Version*, *The New Revised Standard Version*, *The New International Version*, and Eugene Peterson's *The Message*, as well as my own paraphrase. I would suggest that before reading Chapter 6, *Cruciform Wisdom*, you read the first two chapters of First Corinthians in *The Message*.

I hope that it will not prove confusing that sometimes I have used words according to their technical meaning, and at other times I have used the same terms, as have other writers, in a broader and more general sense. For example, when I have wanted to refer to a spiritually transformed personality, a more intuitive way of being which is deeply appreciative of Divine Mystery, I have used the terms *saint*, *mystic*, and *contemplative* somewhat interchangeably. Technically, *contemplation* is prayer which is not vocal or discursive; that is, it is without words, thoughts, or images, and a *contemplative* is one who experiences communion with God through such prayer. *Meditation*, at least in the Western world, is a more discursive spiritual exercise using our imagination, our intellect, and our will. A meditative lifestyle, then, would be one that is deeply thoughtful, reflective, and insightful. A *saint*, as found in Scripture and understood in Protestant thought, is one who whose life is consecrated to God. *Spiritual formation* refers to the practices and disciplines which deepen our faith, further our growth, and facilitate a profound consciousness of that Sacred Presence and Love which enfolds us all.

Mystery, or *Mysterion* in the Greek New Testament, is another word you will frequently find used in this book and in most other literature regarding spirituality. A mystery is a secret known and shared by those who have been initiated into the fellowship. But mystery is not an ordinary secret. It is not like a puzzle where no secret remains once the puzzle has been solved. Nor is it like a mathematical problem that leaves no questions once the answer has been found. The knowledge of mystery leads to ever-deepening questions and insights. It is a secret known more through the faculties of appreciation, wonderment, awe, and trust than it is through ordinary human reason. It's more like seeing the one you love in the lovely shadowing of candlelight than in the harsh glare of a florescent lamp.

Mysticism has been defined in many ways, but simply put has to do with experiencing the infinite mystery and nearness of God first-hand. The Christian *mystic* is a man or woman who has discovered immediate communion with Christ; and in unity with Christ recognizes his or her connection to all others. Having discovered the joy of the dance the mystic seeks to include everyone else, helping people to feel more loved and cared for—especially the poor, the outsider, the powerless, and the dispossessed.

The more you develop an inner feeling for what all these terms have in common, the more you will intuitively understand the meaning of Christian spirituality. In time they may even become to you like great drops of rain to a desert traveler.

I hope that in some way what is written here will help you to be grasped by the immense love of God and, in the words of Thomas Merton, to see "the power of that Love to do you good, and to bring you to happiness."

Now when all the people were baptized, and when Jesus also had been baptized and was praying, the heaven was opened, and the Holy Spirit descended upon him in bodily form like a dove. And a voice came from heaven, "You are my Son, the Beloved, with you I am well pleased."

Jesus, full of the Holy Spirit, returned from the Jordan and was led by the Spirit in the wilderness, where for forty days he was tempted by the devil.

Luke 3:21–22; 4:1–2 (NRSV)

I

Into the Desert

In this glare of brilliant emptiness, in this arid intensity of pure heat, in the heart of solitude, great silence and great desolation, all things recede to distances out of reach, reflecting light but impossible to touch, annihilating all thought and all that men have made to a spasm of whirling dust far out on the golden desert.

Edward Abbey, *Desert Solitaire*

The desert is ancient, silent, and spacious. The desert is a place of complete simplicity where life flourishes by seeking only what is necessary. It is thirsty, but waits with timeless patience for the water to fall from frugal clouds, and responds in joyful beauty and flowering gratitude to the lightest of showers.

This elegant simplicity and order of the desert, its unfathomable quiet, elicit feelings of mystery and invite contemplation. Austere and sparse, unmoving motion, the desert somehow compels us to reflect on the essential questions of our existence: Who am I? What should I do? What does it all mean? Must I live my life in isolation and loneliness or is there One there for me? As we gaze at the land sculpted by burning wind, we can feel an imponderable process that has been at work for eons—the saga of a universe of ineffable beauty, unity, and destiny. In the emptiness, in the heart of solitude, a sacred purpose, peace, and presence envelops us, and God discloses both God's and our identities.

It was in the desert that the sacred name. *Yahweh,* or *I Am That I Am,* was made known to Moses. It was in that lonely place that Moses came to know that he was not alone, that no man or woman is ever alone. It was in the desert that Israel discovered its identity, came to understand what was in its own heart. It was in desert solitude and stillness that Elijah heard God in the thin sound of silence. The prophet Hosea says to the people that in order to rediscover who they are, to know again that they are created in love, for love, and by love, they will have to reenter the desert.[1] Likewise, Jesus' experience in the desert was determinative for him. He emerged from the desert with a message and the course of his life set. Three hundred years later Christian monasticism, as a movement of contemplative wisdom and spiritual power, was born when men and women with a passion for self-surrender to the deeper life in Christ, "showed a preference" for the simplicity, the stillness, the solitude, and the emptiness of the Egyptian desert.

What is essential in the spiritual life is, of course, that we find not a dry and sand-blown country far from any geographical city, but rather a desert place of the heart where spiritual transformation can occur. Lent, with its emphasis on taking spiritual inventory, repentance, renunciation, and preparation for Easter, is just such a desert. In fact, we can appropriately think of the forty days from Ash Wednesday to Easter Sunday as a Lenten desert.

It seems significant that Jesus was led into the desert immediately after his life had been publicly consecrated to God in baptism. Baptism represents a kind of death and resurrection. It is a renunciation of the values of acquisitiveness, of anger, of power and control, of self-deification and disbelief. For the Desert Fathers and Mothers and early monastics the whole of Christian spirituality was summed up in Christ's invitation: "If any of you want to be my disciple, then you must deny yourself, take up your cross, and follow me." In these words the early mystics discovered the core values of Christianity. They discovered that what is of primary importance is to live in the same way that Jesus lived, to love with the same love, and to live with the same peace, the same lack of anxiety and anger, as Jesus. In this text for the desert they understood Jesus to be urging them to practice the art of renunciation, the renunciation of one's false self.

There is a contradiction within all of us. The supreme truth of the Christian religion is that God is absolute love and goodness, but we then live as if that were not at all true. We are torn between two lives, a sort of Jekyll-and-Hyde existence, what Scripture calls the life of the flesh and the life of the spirit—the true self and the false self. Lenten observances have the effect of loosening our grip on our self-fabricated existence, and of dismantling all obstacles to the resurrection life. I like Eugene Peterson's translation of the rest of Jesus' invitation: "Self-help is no help at all. Self-sacrifice is the way, my way, to finding yourself, your true self. What good would it do to get everything you want and lose you, the real you?"[2] Desert spirituality in which we find our true selves is, then, a spirituality of renunciation, of sacrificial love, of self-surrender.

In the human heart there is an innate longing for renunciation or self-surrender. We may experience it as a kind of restlessness or even boredom, which are themselves expressions of the desire for meaning. We may even recognize that we would like to give ourselves to some significant cause. Boredom, it has been pointed out, comes not from having too little to do, but from the belief that what we are doing is without meaning. At one time I pastored a small Mennonite congregation, but one in which we celebrated the Eucharist every Sunday. The elderly woman who had graciously prepared communion for us every week moved away to live with her son and daughter-in-law. No one immediately volunteered to take her place and so for several months I did what she had been doing. But I did not do it graciously. We used the little glass cups for the wine and so it was quite a chore. It was an uninteresting job but one that had to be done and so I did it.

One Sunday morning, as I was getting everything ready, I realized how resentful I was that on top of everything else, on top of the big and exciting and meaningful stuff like preaching, I had this mundane and uninteresting task to complete every week. I had to do it every Sunday and I did it without meaning every Sunday.

But then I heard myself saying in my own mind and heart, "Larry, don't you think that the people who are going to receive communion this morning would rather think that it was prepared in love, with thoughtfulness and in prayerfulness, rather than as a loveless and meaningless chore devoid of any sense of God's grace or presence?" From that moment on I never made the physical preparations for the Eucharist without its being a prayer in which I felt a certain kind of joy and nearness to God. In fact since that epiphany it has been far easier for me to grasp the truth that the smallest and most common events and actions, provided they are done in love and with a sense of cosmic mystery, are never without significance.

My own experience suggests to me, then, that boredom, restlessness, and ennui are expressions of our yearning for something beyond all thought, all imagination, and all restricting definitions—symptoms of our longing for some infinite depth of meaning to which we can freely give ourselves.

Those who have been abused may experience their desire as a sudden and grateful realization that the abuse was not their fault. Or our desire may be experienced as loneliness, as the yearning for genuine companionship, a longing for mutual self-giving love. Sometimes it is experienced as a yielding to inexpressible depths of feeling or heights of ecstasy evoked by great music or upon encountering the astounding beauty of nature—the sun shining through the forest trees, the waves breaking on some cliff and spraying high in the air, the colors of a desert sunset, or the starry sky on a cold night. Frequently the desire for self-surrender is experienced as a sense of overwhelming gratitude.

If you have ever experienced a moment of complete acceptance, or a letting go of a serious problem, or a moment in which you relinquished something that was really hurting you, that moment was a part of your desire for self-surrender. There is in each heart a desire to renounce the whole world and to surrender to the loving and transcendent mystery that is God.

In his book *The Awakened Heart*, Gerald May suggests the following exercise: "Think for a moment about what has prompted you to do what you have done in life. When you have tried to be successful in your studies or work what have you been seeking? When you have wanted to be pleasing, attractive or helpful to others, what have you really been hoping for? Remember some moment in your life when you felt most complete and fulfilled, what did you taste there? Recall also feeling very bad, alone, worthless; what were you missing?"[3] Your memories may be painful or happy or sad or joyful, but whatever they are, stay with them as quietly and as gently as you can. Eventually, beneath all your longings, you will discover that the desire to abandon yourself to the love of God is the ultimate reality not only of your own heart but also of the whole universe.

The secular world, the world that does not see God as inherent in all things, is relentlessly at work undermining our surrender. When holy men and women fled to the desert in the third and fourth centuries it was, in part, to escape any entanglement in the world's sticky and deadly web of dishonesty, violence, manipulation, spiritual confusion, and treacherous mingling of indifference and hostility toward what is sacred and wholesome and truly human. When the Abbot Marcus asked the Abbot Aresenius, "Wherefore do you flee from us?" Aresenius answered, "God knows that I love you, but I cannot be with God and with men— a thousand and a thousand thousand angelic powers have one will, but men have many. Therefore I cannot send God from me and come and be with men."[4]

Without an inner desert to go to far from the seductive city, without an inner place of stillness and prayer, it is impossible to live a life of surrender with any consistency, or to live in non-conformity to the illusory world which promises to satisfy our infinite longing with what is finite. The *Big Book* of Narcotics Anonymous says that in order to recover an addict may have to change his or her playground, playthings, and playmates.

In *The Wisdom of the Desert*, Thomas Merton tells how the Desert Fathers and Mothers regarded society as a shipwreck from which one had to swim for one's life.[5] "These were people who believed that to let oneself drift along, passively accepting the tenets and values of what they knew as society was purely and simply a disaster." However, not only were they fleeing the disaster of society, and the church that had so thoroughly accommodated itself to it, but they also went into the desert to confront demonic power. "For our struggle," writes the apostle Paul, "is not against flesh and blood, but against the rulers, against the authorities, against the powers of this dark world and against the spiritual forces of evil in the heavenly realms."[6] The Christian mystics of the desert felt it necessary to guard against the seductive suggestions of the world and to confront the powers of evil, whether such powers are conceived of as personal and supernatural or as the workings of our own internal pathologies. Either way, there are demons which will appear, and with which we must struggle in the desert—addictive behaviors, destructive beliefs, and hurtful ways of relating to each other. We are a strange mixture of love and hatred.

Each of us must therefore face our own radical sinfulness, our own complicity in the suffering and evil of the world. One time Jesus said to those who were unbelieving that when the Holy Spirit comes, you will be convinced of sin because you do not trust me. This is an important saying because it means that sin is a lack of trust. When Jesus spoke to Pilate of truth, Pilate asked: "What is truth?"[7] His question was not one of philosophical inquiry. It was a biting and cynical commentary on the realities of political life. Pilate was saying something like this: "Jesus, you are an innocent man. You are a wise and good person, a holy person devoted to truth. But of what use is truth and goodness? Today I am going to kill you for no other reason than that it is to the advantage of my political career to do so. Can't you see, Jesus, that brute force and political intrigue are stronger than truth?" That day Pilate chose not to trust the highest ideals of religion or philosophy but to rely instead on his own cunning, and so he sentenced Jesus to death by crucifixion. Whenever we act out of fear or mistrust so that we diminish, or extinguish, the physical or emotional or intellectual or spiritual life of another, that is sin.

Sin may also be thought of as a settled disposition of willfulness rather than willingness; or it may be considered as alienation, which suggests a separation or uprootedness from one's true self, from others, from God. Sin tears asunder the wholeness in which all belongs together. It fails to see the connectedness, the unity, of the cosmos and fractures relationships. There is no sense of God's being "in all things and through all things." It is a failure to see, in the words of Barbara Brown Taylor, that "our life in God is like a luminous web of relationships flung across the vastness of space."[8] The word most frequently translated as *sin* in the New Testament means "to miss the mark" in the same way that an arrow might miss the mark by falling short of the target. Used in this sense sin is a failure to live life according to the best that we can conceive. It is, in fact, to waste our lives. If nothing else, sin is a distraction. I read somewhere that one of the great Hasidic rabbis used to say to his students: "My hope is that you do not sin, not because it is forbidden, but because there is not enough time."

However we conceive of sin, it must be courageously confronted in our own lives. We must face our own demons. So Lent is also a season of repentance.

Repentance is simply a turning of the heart to God. That's all it means. The great religions of the world have all acknowledged the sorry mess that we are in. Buddha said that we suffer because everything is on fire—on fire with passion, infatuation, and hatred. In the first chapter of his Letter to the Romans, Paul describes in lurid detail the envy, deceit, strife, murder, ruthlessness, and arrogance of the human species. But—and I use the word *but*, which means "behold the underlying truth," quite deliberately here—there is a way out. The way out is through radical faith in the love of God as expressed in the historical reality of Christ's death on the cross. In the crucifixion of Christ we feel the powerful love of God moving toward and embracing us. Such an experience dispels our fears, alters our consciousness, heals our metaphysical sickness, and in the deepest places within us it opens up an acute awareness of being loved and of loving. That's repentance. That's contemplation—"a long loving look at God."

The Spirit led Jesus into the quiet desert where he could experience the unconditional love and caring of God, the *Papa* Father and *Amma* Mother, with a deeper and more intense intimacy. And Jesus went willingly into that contemplative place where he abandoned himself in love to Love.

Christian spirituality, then, is the answering of a call. It begins with the overwhelming conviction that we are being invited into a union of love with God through Christ. So perhaps the best way to begin this retreat into the Lenten Desert is not with a lot of strenuous effort, but by simply allowing yourself to relax completely, to center down, and to sit as quietly as you can in the loving presence of God. Don't try to feel anything or to make anything happen. Let go of your problems. Let them float away like a helium-filled balloon. Let everything come to a peaceful standstill. Don't even try to practice some technique of contemplative prayer designed to help you pray without thoughts or images. Insofar as you can, just allow God to love you, and you will discover the secret spring in the desert.

Jesus, full of the Holy Spirit, returned from the Jordan and was led by the Spirit in the wilderness, where for forty days he was tempted by the devil. He ate nothing at all during those days, and when they were over, he was famished. The devil said to him, "If you are the Son of God, command this stone to become a loaf of bread." Jesus answered him, "It is written, 'One does not live by bread alone.'"

Luke 4:1–4 (NRSV)

But Jesus answered, "It is written, 'One does not live by bread alone, but by every word that comes from the mouth of God.'"

Matthew 4:4 (NRSV)

II

Alleluia Is the Song

The climate in which prayer flowers is that of the desert, where the comfort of man is absent, where the secure routines of man's city offer no support, and where prayer must be sustained by God in the purity of faith. Even though he may live in a community, the monk is bound to explore the inner waste of his own being as a solitary. The Word of God which is his comfort is also his distress. The liturgy which is his joy and which reveals to him the glory of God, cannot fill a heart that has not previously been humbled and emptied by dread. Alleluia is the song of the desert.

Thomas Merton, *Contemplative Prayer*

Most of the disciplines of spiritual formation that we find in the Hebrew Scriptures and also in the Gospels, disciplines like solitude, silence, fasting, meditation, prayer, and waiting in quiet stillness, seem to emerge out of a desert spirituality. A desert pilgrimage or a spiritual quest on some wilderness mountain is a frequent theme in Hebrew religion. So Jesus is "led" by the Holy Spirit in the desert where he is tempted, or tested. From a slightly different perspective from that of Luke, the Gospel of Mark says that the Spirit "sent" Jesus out into the desert.[1] Taken together the two accounts suggest that those who go with Christ into the desert are both driven and drawn there.

On the one hand, we may be driven to the desert by our own physical limitations, by illness, injury, or chronic physical pain. We may be driven there by some inner trouble, such as depression or anxiety. The betrayal of a friend or a tumultuous unfulfilling relationship may be the compelling factor. Financial problems or questions of vocation may precipitate a wilderness journey. We may be driven there by the misery of some addiction, by the unmanageability of our lives, by some old and painful wound, or by the sense that we have missed our own life as if we had arrived at the airport late and our plane had left without us.

On the other hand, we may be drawn into the desert by its centering silence, reassuring stillness, and healing emptiness. At some critical juncture in life it may be its clarity and far-ranging visibility that attract us. Like some old prospector persistently searching for the hidden wealth of precious metals we may be drawn to the desert by the promise of ultimate riches, ultimate fulfillment. The desert suggests some mysterious realm beyond itself, some unknown, transcendent reality that we may hope to experience. More than anything else the desert is a call to communion, and we are drawn there, sometimes unconsciously, by the desire to experience the presence of God as God really is in love and truth.

You may want to pause right now to quietly and gently ask what it is that brings you into the Lenten Desert. Are you driven or are you drawn there? The sense of having been sent into the desert can indicate that there is something we need to let go. The feeling that we are being drawn into the desert suggests that what is required is a simple state of relaxation, openness, and receptivity. What is it that gives you a sense of being either sent or drawn into the desert wilderness? In whatever drives or calls you, can you see

16

something more than psychological mechanisms at work? Can you find God in it? Whether we are sent or drawn into the desert, it is to prepare us for some work of love; therefore a third question is, to whom can you show responsible love right where you are?

The story of Jesus' temptation is obviously meant to parallel ancient Israel's experience. The fast of forty days and nights reflects Israel's forty-year wandering in the desert wilderness. Doing without what is normally permitted, fasting as in giving up something for Lent, is meant to symbolize the purity of our intention to be God-conscious. Both Israel's and Jesus' hungers were meant to bring enlightenment and to prepare them for their spiritual work. The preparation of Jesus is accomplished through three critical questions, or decisions. I use the word *preparation* or *test* here because that's the real meaning of *temptation (peirazo)*. In Scripture God's testing is always to be understood in a positive sense. It is meant to reveal previously unknown depths of strength and wisdom, and to make one ready for greater acts of kindness and works of love. Testing that has the Abba Father, the Amma Mother as its source can only have an ever-deepening experience of Love as its intention.

The temptation of Jesus begins and ends with great subtlety: "Since you are the Son of God. . . ." What the tempter calls into doubt is not that Jesus is the Son of God, but what that means. Christian spirituality is so much more than a spiritual high, more than charitable acts, more than church-based help. It is Christ in us. "The Christian," wrote Thomas Merton, "is one whose life and hope are centered in the mystery of Christ. In and through Christ, we become partakers of the divine nature—*divinae consortes natuare*" (2 Pt. 1:4).[2] In our own testing we are confronted with the very same question as Jesus. In what way is Christ the Son of God? Our response determines our spirituality.

The Gospel of John says, "God gave his only begotten Son."[3]

17

And the Nicene Creed declares that Christ is the Son of God, "begotten not created . . . begotten by the Father." To "beget" is to produce or to bring one's progeny, children, race, or kind into existence. In *Mere Christianity* C. S. Lewis pointed out that we only beget something of the same kind as ourselves.[4] Human beings beget human babies, beavers beget beavers, and birds beget birds. However, when we make something, Lewis said, it is of a different kind than ourselves. Beavers beget baby beavers but they build dams. Birds beget baby birds, but they make nests in the trees. Human beings beget human beings but they make computers and paintings. What God begets is God. This is why God is not our Father in precisely the same way that God is Jesus Christ's Father. God is in creation but God's creation is not God. There is that sense in which men and women do not have the same kind of life as God. In Lewis's picture what we do not have in our "fallen" state is "spiritual life—the higher different sort of life that exists in God."[5] The Greeks had two words for *life w*hich are helpful in grappling with this state of things. Our natural or biological life they called *bios*. Spiritual life, the loving overflow of creative energy, they called *zoe*. There is a certain resemblance between the two, but there is also a difference that is larger than the difference between being asleep and awake. Jesus was fully awake and fully alive. The life in Christ was God-life. So the Creed confesses that Jesus the Messiah is the "only begotten" Son of God.

What we are really talking about here is, of course, the Incarnation, the Second person in God becoming one of us—muscle and sinew, bone and blood, heart and mind. This means that because Christ is both truly human and truly God, the divine life is available to us all through Christ. Jesus' purpose, as announced in John's Gospel, was to bring real and full life to our world.

How this infusion of life works no one really knows. The best we can do, in terms of intellectual understanding, is to approach it through imaginative analogy and metaphor. A first step might be to cultivate, with both the ancient mystics and the modern physicists, a consciousness of reality as one instead of as many. Einstein proposed that the whole of physical reality could best be conceived of as a unified field of energy, rather than as a combination of separate fields and particles. More and more the religious and scientific world posits the existence of a universal energy that manifests itself in the physical, mental, and spiritual workings of the cosmos as a whole. We now know that once two subatomic particles have interacted, whatever is done to one will affect the other, even if one is left spinning above the page you are now reading and its twin is sent into a distant galaxy. Not only that, but the response is so instantaneous as to lead us to postulate that the two are not really two, but one. Christian Scripture puts it like this: "There is one God and Father of all, who is above all and through all and in all."[6]

One of the largest and most beautiful of all living things is an aspen grove in Utah's Fish Lake National Forest. The grove covers one hundred and six acres, and has grown by "cloning itself," that is, it has grown by asexual reproduction. Above ground it looks as though there are many separate individual trees. But if you could look beneath the soil, if you could see what is hidden, you would discover that all the trees are fused together by a single complex root system. What appear to be many trees is one living aspen. Whatever might be done, good or bad, to one would affect the whole because in actuality there is only one tree. This helps us to better understand how, in the biblical view, one person, Adam, infected the entire world with death, and how one person, Jesus Christ, inoculated the whole cosmos with life. To quote C. S. Lewis once more: "when Christ becomes human . . . It is as if something which is always affecting the whole human mass begins, at one point, to affect that whole human mass in a new way. From that point the effect spreads through all humankind. It makes a difference to people who lived before Christ as well as to people who lived after Christ. It makes a difference to people who have never heard of Christ. It is like dropping into a glass of water one drop of something which gives a new taste or a new colour to the whole lot. But, of course, none of these illustrations really works perfectly."[7]

Forty days before this, at his baptism by John in the Jordan River, Jesus had an experience that surpasses radical amazement. Eugene Peterson translates Saint Matthew's narrative like this: "The moment Jesus came out of the baptismal waters, the sky opened up and he saw God's Spirit—it looked like a dove—descending and landing on him. And along with the Spirit, a voice: 'This is my Son, chosen and marked by my love, delight of my life.'"[8] But in the desert Jesus hears another voice. "Since you are the Son of God, tell this stone to become bread." Jesus' baptism was an act of humility; it was a sign of his emptying himself of self (Phil. 2:7). Jesus' baptism expressed his total identification with our human plight, and his absolute trust in the goodness of the Father. But the voice Jesus now hears while he is hungry and alone and tired says that since Jesus is the Son of God he surely has the right and the power to satisfy his own needs. Surely the Son of God, full of wonder-working power, should be exempt from human needs such as hunger. It is an especially sinister temptation because there is biblical precedent. God fed the people of Israel with bread, or manna, in the wilderness when they were desperately hungry.

By his reply Jesus refuses to look for "the softer, easier way," which always turns out to be the harder, more difficult way in the end. Nor will he exempt himself from complete and constant dependence on the Father. Jesus' response is based on

20

Deuteronomy 8:2-3:

> And you will remember all the way which the Lord your God
> has led you in the wilderness these forty years, that he might
> humble you, testing you, to know what is in your heart,
> whether you would keep his commandments or not. And he
> humbled you and let you be hungry, and fed you with manna
> which you did not know, nor did your fathers know, that he
> might make you understand that one does not live by bread
> alone, but by everything that proceeds out of the mouth of the
> Lord. (NRSV)

The meaning of Christ's response is not the sweet or socially
acceptable notion that we should not neglect the pursuit of intellectual and spiritual values while taking care of physical needs,
but rather it points down the path of radical reliance on God in
everything. The contemplative path leads to the intuitive recognition that "it is in God that we live, move, and have our very
being." We are all tempted by the illusion that we can take our
lives into our own hands and create our own security. We are
tempted to the belief that if we exercise enough will power, or
if we manage well enough, we can wrest satisfaction, safety, and
even happiness from life. Jesus recognizes this second voice as
an evil voice. It is evil because mistrust, willfulness, and paranoia
regarding our survival needs sap our vital energy. Later Christ will
say, "To do the will of my Father is my food and my drink."

Spiritual life does not come from relying on things or our
effort to save us. It comes from relying on Love. It comes from
taking the word of God into the deepest places within us and becoming one with it. This word is not a series of abstract theological statements or a moral philosophy. It is the living word. It
is the Son of God. It is the Christ. Our true vocation in this life is
to find God. We are to work for the food of eternal life—the
Word, the Logos. "In the beginning was the Word, and the Word
was with God, and the Word was God. He was in the beginning

with God. All things came into being through him, and without him not one thing came into being. What has come into being in him was life, and the life was the light of all people. The light shines in the darkness and the darkness did not overcome it."[9]

What is this eternal Word that is light and life? In the Greek of the New Testament the term *Word* used in Saint John's prologue is *Logos*. The Greeks used it somewhat as we use the word *reason*. One of its first uses was to refer to the word in someone's mind, the reason or intelligence that helps bring some orderly arrangement to life. As the Greek philosophers reflected on the order of the universe, they concluded that there must be some cosmic mind or reason that orders all things, harmonizes all things, and in which all things cohere. John's use of the Greek *Logos* was additionally enriched and extended by his own Jewish understanding of the Hebrew definition of *Word*. The Hebrew expression *davar* could mean either a spoken word or an event. For the ancient Hebrews the *Word*, or *davar*, was a kind of energy, a powerful creative force. God said let there be light, and the primordial darkness was dispelled. The Chinese translation of *Logos*, which really elucidates much of its spiritual meaning, is *Tao*. The *Tao* is the principle underlying and governing the universe. The *Tao* is great beyond naming. The *Tao* "stands alone and does not change. It goes around and does not weary."[10] The word *Tao* is equivalent to both the Greek words *Logos* and *Hodos* (the way), so that in it we can hear echoes of Jesus' saying, "I am the way, and the truth, and the life."[11]

The audacious claim of Christianity is that the Word and the Way, the *Logos* and the *Hodos*, the *Davar* and the *Tao*, were embodied in Jesus of Nazareth. With startling simplicity Saint John says, "And the Word became flesh." More than that, there is Christ's enigmatic saying, "Very truly, I tell you, unless you eat the flesh of the Son of Man and drink his blood, you have no life in you."[12] The question that arises out of all of this, and which calls not just for a rhetorical answer but for a specific and personal response, is: What am I hungry for? What is it that I desire more than anything else? What do I want to desire?

In the sixth chapter of the Gospel of John, after miraculously feeding the five thousand in what John calls the region of Tiberias, but which Luke describes as a "desert" or "uninhabited" place on the northeast side of the Lake of Galilee,[13] Jesus crosses the lake in a storm. When the people find Jesus again on the other side they demand that he give them more bread. They want Jesus to feed them again as he had fed them on that lonely hill near the shore of Galilee. But Jesus wants them to see that he is not just the bread giver, but the bread itself.[14] He explains to them that their ancestors, when they thought they would perish from hunger in the wilderness, were given manna to eat. But the manna, the bread, God provided for them did not sustain them forever. Similarly Jesus, in his concern for their physical hunger, has miraculously given them bread in a rather desolate place, where there is nothing readily available to eat. But now they are hungry again, and the time is coming when even if they are at home with plenty of food of this sort they will, nevertheless, die. But there is another kind of bread, Jesus says, that he would like to give them. And whoever eats this bread will never die. This bread is the bread for which the manna from heaven, and the feeding of the five thousand, is a figure. This bread, the Bread of Life, is Jesus' own person. "I am the living bread that came down from heaven," Jesus says.[15] This is the bread that Jesus longs to give us.[16]

In the bread and wine of Holy Communion, the real, and not just metaphorical, presence of Christ is made available to us. The Bread and Wine are the food and drink that sustain us in the desert. In the Eucharist Christ gives his life, his God-life, to us.

The Lord's Supper is a joint participation in the mystery of the union of Father, Son, and Holy Spirit. It is a mystical union with the love and will of God.

And where do we discover that Christ is our spiritual bread? In the stillness of the inner desert, in the spaciousness of contemplation. In prayer that empties the heart so that it can be filled by the Word. By participating in the mystery of the liturgy, not as an external ritual without soul but as welcoming the embrace of God's presence. How do we overcome despair, addictions, vexatious states of mind, and flaws in our character? By incorporation into Christ. By living in Christ. By a union of love with Christ. By receiving Christ as our life. "The Living God," wrote Merton, "transcendent and immanent, the Alpha and Omega, the beginning and the end, the One who is everywhere and nowhere, makes himself visible and tangible and gives Himself to us to be our spiritual food."[17] Yes! *Alleluia* is the song of the desert.

T hen the devil led him up and showed him in an instant all the kingdoms of the world. And the devil said to him, "To you I will give their glory and all this authority; for it has been given over to me, and I will give it to anyone I please. If you, then, will worship me, it will all be yours." Jesus answered him, "It is written, 'Worship the Lord your God, and serve only him.'"

Luke 4:5–8 (NRSV)

III

The Conjurer

The evil inclination is to be compared to a conjurer who runs among people with a closed hand daring them to guess what is in it. At that moment each one thinks that the conjurer has what each one desires for him or herself hidden in the clenched hand. Everyone therefore runs after him. Once the conjurer stops for a moment and opens his hand there is nothing in it. Exactly does the evil inclination fool the whole world. Everyone rushes after him, for all imagine, in their error, that he has in his hand what they want and desire. In the end the evil inclination opens his hand and everyone sees that there is nothing in it. The very one who said to each person "open your mouth and I will fill it," he himself is completely empty.

Rabbi Nachman of Breslov

The desert is often a place of intense dreams and strange visions. In this second temptation the devil speaks calmly and plausibly of the worship of power, while Jesus stands on top of a majestic mountain where he can see the glory and fascinating possibilities of all the world's political and military might. Here is a visionary experience, which, like all visionary experiences, makes visible the invisible drama of the spiritual realm of demons and of angels and of the human soul.

At least part of what is made visible in Jesus' vision is the temptation of Jesus, and of every man and of every woman, to acquire power through the worship of evil. Rollo May said in his book *Power and Innocence,* "For the living person power is not a theory, but an ever present reality which he or she must confront, use, enjoy, and struggle with a hundred times a day."[1] The desert is where I experience this confrontation most acutely. There in the sound of silence I hear the question: "What do I worship?" Or, to use Paul Tillich's phrase, "What is my Ultimate Concern? What are my values, and how do they relate to my actual use of power? What is the great passion of my life?" Jesus' answer to Satan's offer of world power, if Jesus will only worship him, comes from the sixth chapter of Deuteronomy: "It is written, You shall worship the Lord your God and serve God only." This is a direct quotation of verse thirteen but also certainly alludes to verses four and five: "Hear, O Israel! The Lord is our God, the Lord is one! And you shall love the Lord your God with all your heart and with all your soul and with all your might." Worship is the unrestricted giving of our whole person to God—the conscious and the unconscious, the body and the mind. It is a state of complete surrender to what we value most, and of unconditional loyalty to what we believe promises unconditional fulfillment. Worship is what we relate to, even in the most ordinary details of daily life, as our Ultimate Concern.

Many concerns fill our days. Some concerns have to do with food, shelter, clothing, or our physical health. Most of us have many concerns surrounding marriage and family, or other relationships. There are concerns of work, of the enjoyment of recreation and of beauty. And there are a good many environmental, social, and political concerns that we may have. You are obviously reading this book because you have spiritual concerns. Whatever becomes our Ultimate Concern, whatever we give our whole heart to, determines everything about us. What we love determines what we will do with the twenty-four hours of the day and how we will do it. It determines what we find beautiful, ugly, inspiring, discouraging. When we are sick and tired and don't think we can continue another minute, it's what keeps us going on. It is what brings joy to our heart and purpose to our actions. It determines how creatively we respond to every person and every situation we encounter. Our Ultimate Love is the source of our wisdom, strength, and fulfillment. Jesus said, in effect, love God and your neighbor and everything else will fall into place.[2] It's that simple and that profound. If our faith and our love are misplaced, if our ultimate concern is with success, or personal comfort, or affection, or power, as in Luke's second temptation, then we will surrender unconditionally to its laws no matter what the cost.

Here is an experiment developed by Charles Tart in *Living the Mindful Life*. It is a belief experiment. It is designed to bring to the surface some of our implicit beliefs that we probably would not want to publicly express or own. The experiment consists in reading a statement of belief written in the form of a creed. In fact it directly and intentionally parallels the Apostles' Creed, but in contrast to any Christian creed it reflects the Ultimate Concern of the secular world, especially the concern with power, and the values we have acquired as a result of our cultural conditioning. When you read the following statement, do so out loud and with expression; put energy into it. It might even help if you stand up and at attention to read. After reading sit back down, close your eyes, and pay attention to how you feel physically and emotionally. Don't start arguing with it intellectually; just note how it makes you feel.

The Western Creed

I believe in the material universe as the only ultimate reality, a universe controlled by fixed physical laws and blind chance.

I affirm that the universe has no creator, no objective purpose, and no objective meaning or destiny.

I maintain that all ideas about God or gods, enlightened beings, prophets and saviors, or nonphysical beings or forces are superstitions and delusions. Life and consciousness are totally identical to physical processes and arose from chance interactions of blind physical forces. Like the rest of my life, *my* life and *my* consciousness have no objective purpose, meaning or destiny. I believe that all judgments, values, and moralities, whether my own or others, are subjective, arising solely from biological determinants, personal history, and chance. Free will is an illusion. Therefore, the most rational values I can personally live by must be based on the knowledge that for me what pleases me is good, what pains me is sad. Those who please me or help me to avoid pain are my friends; those who pain me or keep me from my pleasure are my enemies. Rationality requires that friends and enemies be used in ways that maximize my pleasure and minimize my pain.

I affirm that churches have no real use other than social support, that there are no objective sins to commit or be forgiven for, that there is no retribution for sin or reward for virtue other than that which I can arrange, directly or through others. Virtue for me is getting what I want without being caught and being punished by others.

I maintain that the death of the body is the death of the mind. There is no afterlife and all hope of such is nonsense.[4]

Sit for a couple of minutes, noticing your reaction.

Many people feel sad, depressed, anxious, sick, repulsed, or horrified. Yet this creed expresses the way of thinking into which we have been conditioned, and even though such beliefs may be completely antithetical to our consciously held values and concerns, there is a part of us that worships according to the "Western Creed." Although usually stated with more tact than it is here, this creed forms the underlying assumptions of much of our modern society. Tart asks a question worth reflecting on: "If you do believe in God, in some kind of spiritual nature to the universe, do you ever have moments of conflict when you think maybe you are wrong? Maybe your belief is silly? Maybe it is immature? We are all taught that so-called primitives need to believe in God, but aren't we educated people supposed to rise above primitive superstition?"[4] Again, none of this is really new. It is the temptation faced by Jesus in the ancient Palestinian desert and by us every day. It is the temptation to love things and use people, rather than loving people and using things. It is the temptation to embrace the rationalization that the end justifies the means, forgetting that the use of evil means can only result in an evil end. It is the temptation to believe that deceit, violence, suspiciousness, force, and a narcissistic spirit are more powerful than humility, compassion, gentleness, kindness, goodness, simplicity, integrity, faith, and love. It is the temptation to look for something external—money, sexual gratification, applause, or power—to make us happy and to fix whatever may be wrong on the inside.

The Western Creed is based on the premise that happiness can be achieved by controlling people and events. At some level most of us believe that the acquisition of physical power equals satisfaction in life. It may be as Shakespeare's character Jaques says, that all the world's a stage. But if that is true then it seems few of us are content to simply play our little part and move on. Instead we want the leading role and all the best lines. We want to be the writer, producer, and director. If only other people would let us direct them, we would all be much happier. Of course life doesn't follow our script, and the other actors resent our direction. They prefer a freer method of acting and either passively or aggressively resist our efforts to control them. By the final act no one is happy and the whole thing ends in disaster.

I used to think that everything would be okay, and I would be perfectly happy, if I could just get my life arranged in some idyllic way and hold it there. The fact that I was not successful in arranging things meant, to me, that I was not using enough will power, or that I was perhaps being victimized in some way. Eventually I saw that my efforts to control the future were the very source of the problem, that through "willfulness" I was creating my own unhappiness. I was helped immensely by these four lines of William Blake's poetry:

He who binds to himself a joy
Does the winged life destroy,
But he who kisses the joy as it flies
Lives in eternity's sunrise.[5]

"To kiss the joy" is to live with appreciation, acceptance, and love in the present moment. "To kiss the joy" is to live without trying to control the next moment. Perhaps you can think of some time in the past year when you were able to accept everything as it was with a grateful heart, where you felt no need to change or rearrange or possess anything, where you were just living in the moment with grateful acceptance.

This is the *Way* of Holy Scripture, the Way that is Christ. It is the way of a willing, surrendered spirit and a grateful heart. The Way is like water—yielding, yet powerful in its effects. The Way is the path of nonaction, which means not the absence of action but rather acting without artificiality or willfulness. It is acting without compulsiveness and without trying to make something happen. For example, when a family member is addicted to alcohol or drugs it means "detaching in love," recognizing that you cannot control that person's addiction. Certainly it means that we do not "thrive" on someone's dependency on us. The Way is the way of the Hebrew *anawim* (meek) in the Beatitudes of Jesus and in the

Psalms. The meek are the marginalized. The meek have no economic, social, political, or military power. Nevertheless the *anawim* are strong like water, and able to survive with integrity in times of terror and chaos. The *anawim* don't use force, but instead leave an open space where good things can happen. The meek appear, then, to have a preference for what seems like weakness to the secular world, but which turns out to be a supernatural strength.

The question is sometimes asked whether Satan could have or would have given Jesus total world power. There is only space here to point out that the devil is a conjurer. Jesus said that Satan is "a murderer and a liar," the very "father of lies."[6] It's not just that the one hand everyone thinks contains the prize is empty, but that with the other hand, which no one is watching, Satan steals— steals the very essence of our humanity. Jesus does not fall for the illusion. Jesus sees that life is real, authentic, and substantial only insofar as it is centered in God as the source of truth, goodness, and beauty. When I think that I am some "autonomous source of power," then I am under the evil conjurer's spell.

God alone, Jesus says, quoting from Deuteronomy, is to be worshipped. It is entirely possible to believe in God, but not to worship God or to have God as our Ultimate Concern; to live, instead, according to the Western Creed, to live according to the values of a violent, greedy, egocentric society, and never to recognize that contradiction in our lives. There is a stanza in W. H. Auden's poem "The Witnesses" that goes like this:

> Look into your heart and see:
> There lies the answer.
> Though the heart like a clever
> Conjuror or dancer
> Deceive you often into many
> A curious slight
> And motives like stowaways
> Are found too late.[7]

The truth is that not one of us is entirely disinterested in the exercise of power. But in the Lenten Desert we have the opportunity to see the contradictions, to recognize the destructive and manipulative ways in which we are tempted to use power. There our hearts may be purified so that we can see God in the only way God can be seen, by love. Through the disciplines of desert spirituality—prayer, fasting, meditation, contemplation— we allow our hearts to be emptied of all concerns, hopes, and desires so that only God remains as our Ultimate Concern, our ultimate hope, our ultimate desire.

To worship God is to attribute ultimate worth and absolute reality to God. It is to value, more than anything else, God for God's sake. To paraphrase the Quaker philosopher D. Elton Trueblood, when the chief glory of our lives arises from the fact that we have met God, that is spiritual worship.[8] That is really why we go into the desert. We go to meet and worship God as the chief glory of our lives.

Then the devil took him to Jerusalem and placed him on the pinnacle of the temple, saying to him, "If you are the Son of God, throw yourself down from here, for it is written, 'He will command his angels concerning you, to protect you,' and 'On their hands they will bear you up, so that you will not dash your foot against a stone.'"

Jesus answered him, "It is said, 'Do not put the Lord your God to the test.'"

When the devil had finished every test, he departed from him until an opportune time.

Luke 4:9–13 (NRSV)

IV

The Third Test

The desert—the real desert—bears in its physical reality the sign of isolation not only from people and human life, but from any semblance of human presence and activity. Being something that we cannot put to use, it likewise bears the sign of aridity and consequently of the subduing of all the senses, including both sight and hearing. It also bears the sign of poverty, of austerity, and of the most extreme simplicity. In short it bears the sign of humankind's complete helplessness as we can do nothing to subsist alone and by ourselves in the desert, and we thus discover our weakness and the necessity of seeking help and strength in God.

René Voillaume, *Jesus Caritas*

The physical desert is mostly sand and rock and stone and heat. Various plants and living creatures, beautiful and exotic, have made the desert their home, but the desert is largely empty, largely useless and unprofitable from the human point of view. Nor are we likely to find in the Lenten Desert, in the spiritual desert, what can be used for our own personal advantage or profit. Desert places are places of obstacles, places of doubts and paradoxes concerning the presence of God. The desert gives us a sense of the rhythm and essential unity of life, but it may also leave us feeling intensely lonely and isolated; or, at least, aware that we have experienced something very different from ourselves. This seems to be a part of Jesus' desert experience, and the experience of the people of Israel to which the third temptation alludes.

Each of the three temptations of Jesus is meant to be understood as a type of the desert testing undergone by Israel. The third temptation of Jesus, third in Luke's Gospel, is particularly like that of Israel at Massah and Meribah. The people of Israel made their journey through the wilderness to Sinai in stages. By the time they reached Rephidim, which ironically means the place of rest, they were out of water, and to their horror they found that there was no water at Rephidim for either them or their livestock. The situation was desperate. They lost confidence in Moses. In their fear and anger they accused Moses of trying to murder them and their children: "You have brought us up from Egypt," they growled, "to kill us and our children and our livestock with thirst."[1] The seriousness of the situation is seen in Moses' fear that they were about to stone him to death, a form of death that would signify the total repudiation of his spiritual and prophetic leadership and, therefore, of God also. God then miraculously provided water. But how water was provided is not the point of the story. The point of the story, and its connection with Jesus' temptation, is found in its brief conclusion: "Moses named the place Massah and Meribah, because the Israelites quarreled and tested the Lord, saying, 'Is the Lord among us or not?'"[2] Years later, at the end of his life, Moses urged the people to remember this incident as a guiding experience, to remember it as a part of their collective spiritual wisdom. "Do not put the Lord your God to the test," he said, "as you tested him at Massah."[3] This temptation involves two elements: "quarreling" and "testing."

To these people the cities of Egypt were familiar; they therefore seemed comfortable and secure even if they were prisons. By contrast, the desert is unfamiliar, alien, and hazardous. Their quarrel arises from this very experience of the desert as austere and foreign. The Jungian analyst Robert Johnson describes the human psychological journey as one that moves in stages from an innocent wholeness in which the inner and outer world are one, to a separation and differentiation between the inner and outer worlds in which there is a sense of life's duality, and then, at last, to enlightenment, a conscious reconciliation of the inner and outer worlds in harmonious wholeness. "But," Johnson asserts, "we have no right to talk about the last stage, until we are aware of our separateness and duality. We can do all manner of mental acrobatics and talk of the unity of the world; but we have no chance of functioning in this manner until we have succeeded in differentiating the inner and outer worlds. We have to leave the Garden of Eden before we can start the Heavenly Journey. It is ironic that the two are the same place but the journey must be made."4 Or, to use the images from Exodus, we have to be able to recognize the difference between the cities of Egypt and the simplicity of the desert. Perhaps we would be more correct in saying that we must recognize the duality of the desert before we can experience its unity, that "being at one" where, in Gerald May's words, "preoccupations, misgivings, worries, and desires all seem to evaporate, leaving everything perfect just as it is."5 Since everything, including God, is eventually made to serve our own felt-needs and whims, the use of magic is actually a subtle, or not so subtle, attempt to be our own Higher Power.

Especially in the Gospel of Mark we see this duality, these two sides to the desert. Jesus is tempted by Satan and is with wild animals, but he is also cared for by angels. Mark brings together, then, symbols of danger, chaos, and destruction with a symbol of divine presence and care. In the desert we encounter not only the unity but also the otherness of things, troubles that are not of our own manufacturing. In life we meet beasts and monsters that are real and not just products of our own imagination, or the manifestation of individual psychological processes.

It is in the honest grappling with our own internal passions and the external hostilities of life that our mature identity is forged, so that the real self can be surrendered to Christ and united to God. Quite often it is the realization that the world is not always a nice place that awakens our spiritual consciousness. It is frequently some personal experience of alienation, injustice, or suffering that makes us aware of what is greater than ourselves. As we face life's serious and very real difficulties in simple prayer, wordless contemplation, and quiet meditation on sacred Scripture, our center of meaning shifts from self-consciousness to Christ-consciousness. "It is no longer I who live," writes Saint Paul, "but it is Christ who lives in me."[6] In the contemplative desert we discover that happiness is not the object of life. To live in conscious love toward God and others is the object of life. Indeed, happiness remains elusive until the moment we quit chasing it and recognize that real happiness—meaning that happiness which does not depend on what happens—is not an end in itself but a result of communion with Christ.

There can be no genuine unitive experience with its accompanying joy or ecstasy that denies temptation or leaves suffering out. In the desert Jesus did not deny the reality of his temptation but faced it in total openness to the truth. Jesus' spirituality did not leave suffering out, but rather embraced every circumstance and event of life with an attitude of faith, hope, and love.

I am reminded by this whole issue of self-discovery and identity of that wonderful poem written by the German pastor and theologian Dietrich Bonhoeffer shortly before his execution:

Who am I? They often tell me
I stepped from my cell's confinement
calmly, cheerfully, firmly,
like a *Squire* from his country house.

Who am I? They often tell me
I used to speak to my warders
freely and friendly and clearly,
as though it were mine to command.

Who am I? They also tell me
I bore the days of misfortune
equitably, smilingly, proudly,
like one accustomed to win.

Am I then really that which other men tell of?
Or am I only what I myself know of myself?
Restless and longing and sick, like a bird in a cage,
struggling for breath, as though hands were compressing my
    throat,
yearning for colours, for flowers, for the voices of birds,
thirsting for words of kindness, for neighbourliness,
tossing in expectation of great events,
powerlessly trembling for friends at an infinite distance,
weary and empty at praying, at thinking, at making,
faint, and ready to say farewell to it all.

Who am I? This or the Other?
Am I one person today and tomorrow another?
Am I both at once? A hypocrite before others,
and before myself a contemptible woebegone weakling?
Or is something within me still like a beaten army
fleeing in disorder from victory already achieved?

Who am I? They mock me, these lonely questions of mine.
Whoever I am, Thou knowest, O God, I am thine![7]

Bonhoeffer, in his personal desert, was able to bring everything together in a harmonious whole. He understood how his true identity was determined by self-surrender to Christ.

So who are you? How have you used hardship, difficulty, suffering to become a more generous, loving, deeper man or woman? Have you been able to embrace all the events of your life, the good and the bad, with some kind of appreciation and gratitude?

The second issue in this temptation for both Israel and Jesus is focused by the question "Is the Lord among us or not?" We experience real financial hardship and we want to know, "Is the Lord present or not?" We are betrayed by family or treated like strangers by friends and we want to know, "Is the Lord present or not?" Our marriage is a disaster and we want to know, "Is the Lord present or not?" Our children are in serious trouble and we want to know, "Is the Lord present or not?" Everything seems to conspire to defeat us. There is illness, accident, and death and we want to know, "Is the Lord present or not?" There is absolutely nothing wrong with asking that question. Asking the question is not a testing of God. Testing God has to do with trying to force God to show or prove God's self on our terms. "If you're Jesus Christ," the character of Herod sings to a wicked boogie beat in *Jesus Christ Superstar*, "then walk across my swimming pool." Testing God is an attempt to coerce God into acting in order to determine whether God is present. At Massah the people were in effect saying, "If we are to believe that God is powerfully and lovingly present, then God must show us by giving us, and our herds and flocks, water to drink here in the desert, right now." This is precisely Jesus' temptation, the temptation to force God's hand, to make God act in order to demonstrate divine presence, power, and caring.

The Cistercian monk Thomas Keating sees this as a temptation to pursue fame and public esteem.[8] If all the people gathered in the temple courts see Jesus jump from the pinnacle without injury, they will be utterly astonished. Jesus will have

42

their complete admiration. He will be "Jesus Christ, *Superstar!*" Keating views the three temptations as three self-centered programs for happiness that have been built up around our instinctual needs and have become energy centers. The first temptation, to turn the stone to bread, addresses Jesus' need for security and survival, which constitutes the first energy center. The second temptation in Luke, the temptation of power over people and events, "is the last ditch effort to achieve its own invulnerability and immortality." Affection and esteem needs, according to Keating, constitute the center of gravity of the energy system manifested in Luke's third temptation. Others have seen each of the three temptations as an attempt to lure Jesus into taking a shortcut in his work, which in the end would have the effect of derailing his Messianic mission. If Jesus will turn stones to bread, just think of what that could mean in terms of alleviating human hunger and building a following. If Jesus will accept Satan's offer to invest him with worldly power, imagine the good Jesus could do. If Jesus will establish himself as a "wonder worker" who cannot be hurt or killed, think of what a formidable army could be raised. It is certainly true that in each of the temptations Jesus must choose what kind of messiah he will be. Will he turn the stone to bread and relieve his own hunger, or will he give himself as bread for the whole world? Will Jesus attempt to build the kingdom of light through evil means, or will he overcome injustice, violence, and hatred with simplicity, humility, and truth? Certainly each of the three temptations can be understood as an evil attempt to subvert Jesus' self-emptying, self-surrendering attitude. The account of Jesus' temptation is probably polyvalent; that is, it has different meanings, all of them true, depending on who is reading the account and the circumstances under which he or she is reading it.

The critical question is, how do you see the temptation of

Jesus re-enacted in your own life? What are your own mistaken programs for personal happiness? Where and how in your life do you experience the third temptation? For me personally, The Third Temptation is wrapped up in an attempt to manipulate God for my own purposes and assurance. This also seems to me to be an interpretation that is consistent with the text.

The temptation to manipulate God is the temptation to rely on magic rather than on the support of the Holy Spirit. It represents a pathological use of religion. It is a diseased spirituality. By magic I mean the effort to control events or to produce effects through religious or psychological incantations, charms, obsessions, rituals, and legalisms. Underlying the magical use of religion is the belief that every event is determined totally by God, that there is no such thing as something being an accident, or of there being a chance of more than a single outcome for any situation. In magical thinking there is no such thing as the coexistence of accident and chance with a divinely predetermined course. The underlying assumption of magic is that if we will perform the right act, in the right way, and at the right time we can perfectly understand and manage all hidden purposes. As Wayne Oates writes in *When Religion Gets Sick*, "Thus everything becomes controllable, and every outcome is predictable; we can be secure because what is going to happen has been decided by our behavior. We have nothing to worry about now. The risks of the future have been charted, precautions taken, and we are safe."[9]

We all want to feel safe. We would all like to be free of the frightening uncertainties that come upon us in the night. We would like to know that the decision we are about to make is the right one. We would like some relief from the anxiety that comes from living in a universe where there is so much that is unpredictable. And so we turn to magic, to the magic of fundamentalism, astrology, psychology, or scientific determinism. Whether we are theological liberals or conservatives, highly sophisticated or terribly unsophisticated, educated or illiterate, we all face the temptation to escape the ambiguities and dangers of life through magical thinking. In the end, however, the only thing we really escape is the joy of our own freedom.

Magical religion, false spirituality, says: believe, pray, and read your Bible in a certain way, rigidly live your life according to a prescribed legal formula, and you can take all the unpredictability, ambiguity, and risks out of life. The mature religious sentiment, real spirituality, instead calls for us to have the faith and courage, like Abraham, to move beyond the familiar edges of the known, to accept the risks of a desert adventure.

Our technological society is obsessed with the acquisition of information because it believes that the more we know about something the more easily and fully it can be controlled. A client of mine, suffering from severe anxiety, was obsessed with the idea that she had to think of everything, had to know everything, at once, otherwise there might be a death in her family. Obviously this obsession served only to increase and perpetuate her already intolerable anxiety. None of the standard clinical interventions helped, and medication was problematic because of drug addiction. But one day she came in calmer and more relaxed than I had ever seen her. When I asked what had happened she said, "I got so tired that I decided it was easier to just let things happen and trust God that I will be okay no matter what." There is something better than control, better than magic, and that is trust in God as ever present and caring, and inexhaustibly compassionate.

But how are we to be sure that God is present? How can we best handle the temptation to manipulate God into making his presence known, as if that were actually possible? Many of the great saints and mystics have taught that we know God by a kind of unknowing. Since God transcends all our images, definitions, and in-

45

tellectual explanations, it is best to empty our minds of all conceptual knowledge of God and to simply be with God in the deep silence and vast emptiness of the desert. When we abandon all our mind games, when there is a great stillness of body, mind, and heart, it is like being alone in the purifying desert on a night with no moon. It is like being encompassed in a thick cloud of unknowing, and there in the mind, void of discursive reasoning, there in that bright darkness, love begins to stir, and it is that love which is the knowledge of God. Fall in love with God and that will decide everything else. It will guide you through every temptation. Love is the flower that blossoms most beautifully in the desert, and in love God discloses both God's and our mysterious identity.

Then Jesus went with them to a place called Gethsemane; and he said to his disciples, "Sit here while I go over there and pray." He took with him Peter and the two sons of Zebedee, and began to be grieved and agitated. Then he said to them, "I am deeply grieved, even to death; remain here, and stay awake with me." And going a little farther, he threw himself on the ground and prayed, "My Father, if it is possible, let this cup pass from me; yet not what I want but what you want." Then he came to the disciples and found them sleeping; and he said to Peter, "So, could you not stay awake with me one hour? Stay awake and pray that you may not come into the time of trial; the spirit indeed is willing, but the flesh is weak." Again he went away for the second time and prayed, "My Father, if this cannot pass unless I drink it, your will be done. Again he came and found them sleeping, for their eyes were heavy. So leaving them again, he went away and prayed for the third time, saying the same words. Then he came to the disciples and said to them, "Are you still sleeping and taking your rest? See, the hour is at hand and the Son of Man is betrayed into the hands of sinners. Get up, let us be going. See, my betrayer is at hand."

Matthew 26:36–46 (NRSV)

V

The Place of the Oil Press

We are called upon to live Christ's life. We are called into the desert to meet the demon within. We are called to face God alone in the night of our solitude. We are called to die with Jesus, in order to live with Him. We are asked to lose all, to be emptied out in order to be filled with the very fullness of God.

James Finley, *Merton's Palace of Nowhere*

An old olive orchard with its spring blossoms caressed by the soft darkness of the night, and so near the safe walls of the city and the sanctuary of the temple, seems far removed in place or thought from any desert. Yet the very name of this spot, Gethsemane, meaning "the place of the oil press," tells us that it is not only a garden but also a deep desert of the soul. It is into this "garden-desert" that Jesus goes with his disciples and friends on Passover night, and where Jesus prays with such intensity that his sweat is like drops of blood squeezed from his body.

Jesus leads the disciples to what is perhaps a secret place in the garden, and tells most of them to sit, to remain there. I do not think it is at all presumptuous for us to assume that their sitting is to be a time of reflecting meditatively on all the mysterious and enigmatic sayings from earlier in the evening at supper.

So Jesus tells the eight to sit meditatively while he continues on a little ways with Peter, James, and John. Here, in this place of the oil press, it becomes obvious to these three that Jesus is sad and troubled, pressed to the point that it feels like death. The word troubled has to do with a sort of restlessness in the face of some great difficulty that cannot be escaped or evaded. It may be that Jesus' trouble and sorrow have to do with his own impending death. But when I think of all the ordinary people who have faced their death with such gentleness and serenity, it is difficult for me to believe that the prospect of personal physical death alone could agitate Jesus this much. Some think that Jesus' death entailed a spiritual separation from the Father, and it is this imminent separation that is Christ's agony in Gethsemane. Others think that it is the temptation to despair, to the belief that he has failed to awaken the world to God's love. Somehow taking the suffering and sin of the world upon himself was certainly a part of his agony. After reading Henri J. M. Nouwen's *Can You Drink the Cup?*, I am convinced that this test has to do with following the way of unconditional self-giving love in blind faith.[1] The earthly Jesus was not all knowing. Although Jesus was God with us, Jesus was not, in the words of J. B. Phillips, "God pretending to be human."[2] Jesus lived by faith and died by faith—faith that our salvation is in love, through love, and by love. Nevertheless, in the last analysis, it is impossible to know what depths of suffering-love a soul as great as Christ's might experience.

This should not be terribly surprising to us. Most of us have experienced troubles and sorrows that are too deep for words, or perhaps even some test of the soul that is ultimately unnamable. Faced with deep sorrow and trouble Jesus does not become frantic and act rashly or inappropriately. He gathers his friends together so that they can draw strength from one another. He tells them to sit together in quiet meditation. After taking Peter, James, and John a little farther Jesus urges them to wait, watch, and pray while he goes on alone, at least metaphorically, to the olive press itself. The apocalyptic moment approaches. Preparations must be made.

The truth is that Jesus' whole life was a preparation for this moment. If our desire is for spiritual transformation, then we too must take our preparation as seriously as Jesus did. Dallas Willard, in his intriguing book The Spirit of the Disciplines, has pointed out that most Christians think that the beauty of Jesus' life is seen in that he simply made the right choices whenever under pressure. Following Christ is seen as trying to behave as Christ would in the face of an important situation. Willard says of this approach to following Christ, "It is part of the misguided and whimsical condition of humankind that we so devoutly believe in the power of effort-at-the-moment-of-action alone to accomplish what we want and to completely ignore the need for character change in our lives."[3] M. Scott Peck writes along similar lines: "There are many people I know who possess a vision of [personal] evolution yet seem to lack the will for it. They want, and believe it is possible, to skip over the discipline, to find an easy shortcut to sainthood."[4] Without the insight and strength that only the spiritual disciplines can provide, our efforts to control our behavior at the critical moment are doomed to fail miserably.

The secret is to learn how to follow the preparations, the same spiritual disciplines, that enabled Jesus to act with so much wisdom, love, joy, and strength. It is not that practicing disciplines like worship, prayer, sacred reading, meditation, and contemplation is a way of making ourselves spiritual, or of creating an experience of God as Mystery and Love, but that they can open us to the transforming work of the Spirit and to the presence of God.

Prayer, the asceticism of the desert, was neither sporadic nor random with Jesus. According to the Gospels his life was characterized by a set of spiritual disciplines, by a coherent rule of life. In spiritual theology a rule is a systematic pattern of prayer and worship. It is a personal ascetical program or composition of exercises. If we want to have the same insight into life that Christ had, if we want to love in the same way that Christ loved, if we want to be aroused by life in the same way as Christ, if we want to experience God as closer and more real than the air in our own lungs or the blood in our veins, then we need a rule of life. What is your rule of life? What is your specific spiritual program? Here in Gethsemane the counsel, the rule that Jesus gives his closest followers is: wait, watch, pray.

The spirituality of the desert, of the Lenten Desert, is fundamentally a condition of waiting. So Psalm 62 says, "For God alone my whole being waits in silence." Waiting means not seeing, not knowing, not having, not possessing. T. S. Eliot wrote in "East Coker":

> Shall I say it again? In order to arrive there,
> To arrive where you are, to get from where you are not,
> You must go by a way wherein there is no ecstasy.
> In order to arrive at what you do not know
> You must go by a way which is the way of ignorance.
> In order to possess what you do not possess
> You must go by the way of dispossession.
> In order to arrive at what you are not
> You must go through the way in which you are not.
> And what you do not know is the only thing you know
> And what you own is what you do not own
> And where you are is where you are not.[5]

Eliot's poem is an eloquent expression of desert spirituality, of the apophatic tradition of waiting in emptiness, waiting in wordless and imageless prayer to encounter the God who is beyond mere belief.

Waiting is not possessing. In Romans Saint Paul writes, "But hope that is seen is no hope at all. Who hopes for what he already has? But if we hope for what we do not yet have, we wait for it patiently."[6] This kind of waiting is that poverty of spirit which Jesus describes in the Beatitudes, a realization that we really can't own or control anything. We can't possess God. God is always an incalculable mystery beyond us. And given the provisional and highly tenuous nature of our existence, we certainly can't possess ourselves. Our knowledge is so confused and obviously fragmentary that it can hardly be said that we possess any comprehensive understanding of God, ourselves, others, or the universe. And so we wait in poverty and ignorance, and that poverty enables us to see with a little more clarity the true meaning and value of things. We wait in the darkness of ignorance, and the darkness becomes our light. To the self-righteous religious leaders of his day Jesus said, "If you were blind, you would have no sin; but since you say, 'We see,' your sin remains." If we are blind and we know we are blind, then we see. If we know that we do not know God, who is Infinite Mystery, and if we wait patiently for God to self-disclose to us in love, then we do know something of the mind of God, but more importantly we are known and warmly embraced by the God who is our mother and our father.

We say that waiting means not possessing or having, but paradoxically it also means we have what we are waiting for. In Romans 8 the Apostle Paul says that we are "waiting out our adoption as the children of God."[6] But earlier in that same chapter Paul has said that we are already the sons and daughters of God. Which is it? Are we now the children of God; or, are we still waiting to become God's children? Theologians refer to this as the paradox of "the already and the not yet." This strange formula simply means that we are beginning to experience here and now, what will be. When we wait in hope, the future becomes a present reality to us.

God is therefore known in contemplative emptiness, in receptive stillness, and in quiet simplicity. Waiting leads to the kind of enlightenment that frees us from ego-centeredness and selfish living. Silently, patiently, waiting creates freedom and space, and makes room in our heart for the presence of the Holy Spirit. And it generates an inner calm that allows answers and decisions to emerge freely like the unfolding of a desert rose. Sometimes resort is made to the analogy of a pool of water. If the water pool is turbulent and muddy, then you cannot see anything reflected on its surface, and neither can you see into its depths. If, however, the water is calm and clear, you can see deeply into the pool, and at night the moon will be reflected in the water with such clarity that it will look like a painting. What this means is that spiritual waiting is not waiting for something to happen, but rather it is waiting for and in the tranquility of God's presence. I like Nan Merrill's rendering of verse seven of Psalm 62: "In the Silence rests my freedom and my guidance . . . my refuge is in the Silence."[7] Can you let the turbulence cease before taking action? Can you wait silently in the empty desert, possessing nothing, holding on to nothing?

We wait and we watch. Jesus urges wakefulness, spiritual vigilance. It is not good to fall asleep during any test, especially one that involves questions of life and death. "Stay alert," Jesus says to the sleepy Peter, James, and John, "be in prayer so that you don't wander into temptation without ever knowing you are in danger. There is a part of you that is eager, ready for anything in God. But there's another part that's as lazy as an old dog sleeping by a fire."[8]

Proverbs 4:23 comes to mind as particularly relevant to this matter of watchfulness. It reads like this: "Above all else, guard your heart, for it is the wellspring of life" (NIV). In saying that the heart is the wellspring of life, the writer simply means that it is the source of our thoughts, emotions, and behaviors. If he had been using the language of depth psychology the writer might have spoken of the unconscious as the primeval womb in which the conscious mind, with its capacity for orderly thought, reasoning, feeling, and awareness, was formed. Although every one of us has an inner life, we are tempted to sleep, to live as if there is no unconscious, no inner realm of the soul. We deny our unconscious motivations, rationalize our hurtful and unloving ways of treating other people—often those who are closest to us—and live as if focusing on externals alone can make us happy. Every addiction, whether to a chemical substance, a person, money, power, sex, or anything else, is based on the false assumption that we can find ultimate fulfillment and happiness by ignoring our inner life and fixating on the external, material world.

By denial I do not mean that people reject the concept of the unconscious as factual, but that if they reject it, they reject the inner spiritual realm as being relevant to their own personal lives. I have met many alcoholics who are quite willing to say, "I am an alcoholic." Nevertheless their addictive drinking continues unabated. They don't deny that they are alcoholic; what they deny is that alcoholism is personally relevant to them. They deny the poverty and unmanageability of their lives, and the possibility that they could be "restored to sanity" through surrender to "a power greater than themselves."

Watching is a matter of observing ourselves and examining our motivations through Scripture, prayer, meditation, and worship in which God, if we are open and rigorously honest, reveals us to ourselves. Watchfulness is prayerful introspection. How do my passions—like anger, for example—distract me from my communion with God? How does the inability to forgive prevent the healing of my emotional injuries? Do I show kindness to other people because Christ has transformed me into someone who loves unconditionally and responsibly, or is my kindness really a symptom of my own neurosis as I compulsively attempt to fill the void in my life through other people? Am I loving and serving God as I claim, or am I seeking to enhance my image as a spiritual person? We are therefore encouraged to stay awake and watch, not only by Jesus but by all the great saints and mystics who have spoken of their own desert struggle in seeking that purity of heart so necessary for those whose greatest longing is to see God.

A favorite excerpt of mine is this one from Wordsworth's "Lines Composed a Few Miles above Tintern Abbey." It's about watching, not watching as introspective prayer, but watching for mystery and ineffable presence. To me it speaks of watching for and finding God in all things.

> For I have learned
> To look on nature, not as in the hour
> Of thoughtless youth; but hearing oftentimes
> The still, sad music of humanity,
> Not harsh nor grating, though of ample power
> To chasten and subdue. And I have felt
> A presence that disturbs me with the joy
> Of elevated thoughts; a sense sublime
> Of something far more deeply interfused,
> Whose dwelling is the light of setting suns,
> And the round ocean and the living air,
> And the blue sky, and in the mind of man,
> A motion and a spirit, that impels
> All thinking things, all objects of all thought,
> And rolls through all things.[9]

By sleeping, Peter, James, and John have betrayed Jesus before the police and "death squad" ever enter the garden. They have betrayed Jesus by not remaining present with him. Being present is essential to all spiritual practice. Apart from the ability to be present to God and one another there is no depth of life. So they have also betrayed themselves. By sleeping they have missed the presence of God and the strengthening of the angels that we read about in Luke's depiction of what happened there at Gethsemane, the place of the oil press.

To be awake and alert is to watch for our own inner desire for Love and Mystery. For although we may not be aware of it, although it may be repressed, or distorted, or even mistaken as the desire for something else, we all have deep within us the longing for the transcendent experience of God. Our spiritual progress depends on watching, identifying, and nurturing the deepest and truest desire of our heart.

You might think about your own desires. Is there some way that your lesser desires point to some greater longing beyond themselves? When do you feel the most happy and content?

Wait, watch, pray. There is perhaps no greater New Testament epistle to read on prayer than Philippians, particularly chapter four, verses four through nine. There Paul writes about how prayer supports a life of joy and peace, a life free of anxiety and anger. Actually Paul writes about not one but several ways of praying.

Prayer is, of course, more than words. It is a continual attitude of openness and receptivity to God. The ancient Chinese sage Lao Tzu wrote of wise and holy people who were simple and shapeable like an uncarved block of wood, and as receptive as a hollow cave or a valley.[10]

Supplication is the acknowledgment of our powerlessness to control all of life. It is understanding that no matter how well we manage we can never get everything arranged to our total satisfaction or happiness. It is the recognition of our utter dependence on God, "In whom we live, move, and have our very being."

Petition is asking God for what we need. It's not telling God how to go about meeting our need, but it is asking for God's light and goodness. It's turning to God when we realize that "only a power greater than ourselves can restore us to sanity."

Meditation is the pondering of something in our heart. It is turning things over and over again in our mind, repeating something again and again, chewing on truth like a dog chews on a bone. It's sitting quietly with a holy word or phrase of Scripture until we completely absorb its meaning. Paul's encouragement is to reflect on beautiful things, good things, true things until we take them into the deepest places within us and they can no longer be separated from who we are.

At some point meditation may become contemplation, in which the words gently drop away and all thinking ceases. Contemplation has been described as "a long loving look at God." It is, of course, impossible to sit without any thoughts or mental pictures of any kind, but what one can do is to let all thoughts and images float by without grabbing on to them. Each time something appears on the screen of the consciousness the contemplative lets it go and returns to his or her intention to silently be with God in the stillness of the desert. In this way we may come to experience a quiet exultation and the loveliness of Christ.

All of the above is prayer. What you might like to do now is to consider the various elements of your own prayers, and to identity the ways in which you pray. Do you find that you are drawn to any particular way of praying? What does it mean to you when you hear the saying "Prayer is to spirituality what original research is to science"?

Jesus repeats essentially the same prayer three times. However, when Matthew 26 is read in the original Greek, a certain spiritual progression can be seen. Verse forty-two is more definite than verse thirty-nine that it is not possible for this "cup" to pass. The "Thy will be done" of verse forty-two is also more emphatic than that of verse thirty-nine. Repetition in prayer can have two effects. If it is done mechanically it leads to dullness and boredom. If it expresses the truth of the heart it increases understanding and deepens love. Jesus' repetition brings greater conviction about what is God's will, and what must now be done. When in this kind of prayerfulness we turn our entire being to God, then God's peace can be released into our lives—the kind of peace that "passes all understanding," the kind of peace that no human being can ever create or explain.

When Jesus returns to the sleeping Peter, James, and John for the third time, it is simply too late for them to make preparations. The critical moment has arrived and they are not ready. But the testing of Jesus, his own waiting, watching, and praying, has resulted in even greater spiritual power, as seen in how gentle Jesus is with the betrayer and with the enemies who have come for him with swords and clubs. The time is coming, perhaps many times are coming, when we will be severely pressed and tested. So wait, watch, and pray.

W*e proclaim Christ crucified...Christ the power of God and the wisdom of God....*

When I came to you, brothers and sisters, I did not come proclaiming the mystery of God to you in lofty words or wisdom. For I decided to know nothing among you except Jesus Christ, and him crucified. And I came to you in weakness and in fear and in much trembling. My speech and my proclamation were not with plausible words of wisdom, but with a demonstration of the Spirit and of power, so that your faith might rest not on human wisdom but on the power of God.

Yet among the mature we do speak wisdom, though it is not a wisdom of this age or of the rulers of this age, who are doomed to perish. But we speak God's wisdom, secret and hidden, which God decreed before the ages for our glory. None of the rulers of this age understood this; for if they had, they would not have crucified the Lord of glory....

"For who has known the mind of the Lord so as to instruct him?" But we have the mind of Christ.

1 Corinthians 1:23, 24; 2:1–8, 16 (NRSV)

VI

Cruciform Wisdom

"Were you there," asks the old hymn, "when they crucified my Lord?"
Where are you now in relation to the cross? What do you make of it,
what does it make of you, what do you think, feel, wonder, hope, fear,
know? Because no theology, no work of art, no choral passion or cate-
chism can finally make sense out of it all for you or for me. Our job, on
Good Friday, is simply to sit here, to stand here, to kneel here before this
cross and to enter into our own living encounter with it—with the in-
strument of death, this tree of life, this living, dying Lord—so that when
all is said and done, it is we, good friends in Christ, it is we ourselves
who are the living breathing explanation of it all, the ongoing inter-
preters of what Christ means to this world in which we live—the world
in which for love, he died. Amen.

Barbara Brown Taylor, *God in Pain*

The crucifixion is a desert—a lonely, empty, brutally harsh
desert. But just as there is beauty in the severity and ruggedness
of the desert, so there is indescribable beauty in the passion of
Christ: just ask any artist. All suffering is a desert, and there is no

suffering without its beauty. Neither is there any suffering without wisdom. It is certainly possible for us to miss the beauty and the wisdom of Christ's suffering and death, just as it is entirely possible for us to miss the meaning of our own suffering and death, but this merely points to our own inner need for enlightenment, and not to the absence of goodness, or of truth, or of beauty in the midst of pain.

But in order to see we have to look, we have to be open to insight, receptive to revelation. Writer Edward Abbey described how when he stood in the desert at Arches National Monument in Utah, "gaping at the spectacle of rock and cloud and sky and space" he was filled with a desire "to know it all." Abbey wrote of his wilderness sojourn, "I am here not only to evade for a while the clamor and filth and confusion of the cultural apparatus, but also to confront, immediately and directly if possible, the bare bones of existence, the elemental and fundamental, the bedrock which sustains us. I want to be able to look into a juniper tree, a piece of quartz, a vulture, a spider, and see it as it is in itself, devoid of all humanly ascribed qualities, anti-Kantian, even in the categories of scientific description." Abbey said that what he wanted there in Utah's Moab Desert was to meet God face to face.[1] This is somewhat like the mysticism of Lent, where we come to enlightenment by a long inner gaze at the cross in the desert.

In the spirituality of Saint Paul, particularly as we find it expressed in the Corinthian correspondence, Christ is "the wisdom of God and the power of God." There Paul emphasizes that Christ is the one "whom God made our wisdom." In the Old Testament literature the creative energy by which the universe is created is sometimes attributed to the word of God and sometimes to the wisdom of God. Passages like Psalm 33:6 and Proverbs 8:22–31 parallel John's description of Jesus as the Word, or *Logos*, so that we can say that Jesus is the Christ, the Son of God, the

Word of God, and the Wisdom of God. But what a strange, strange wisdom this is to be crucified on a cross.

To the Greeks, meaning those who go in for a purely intellectual wisdom, and to the Jews, those people who regardless of their ethnic group are looking for some dramatic display of power, "the Message that points to Christ on the cross seems like sheer silliness."[2] To both ways of thinking the crucifixion of Christ is so weak, so absurd, so powerless, so foolish and unintelligible that it is impossible to give it serious consideration. Their egocentric thinking demands that God submit to their criteria for truth and right living. However, what Saint Paul demonstrates in First and Second Corinthians is that God's cruciform power and wisdom transcends all human standards of evaluation.

In general the people of ancient Corinth, like people in many modern cities, were obsessed with self-regarding aspirations. They spent a lot of time promoting themselves. They put a lot of effort into dominating situations and people. They understood all about trying to gain "leverage." They admired rich celebrities who had the power to be obnoxiously rude and aggressive. They would have responded positively to the "health and prosperity gospel" proclaimed by some so-called preachers. They would have had a keen interest, as do many people today, in any program guaranteeing success. They would have had enormous respect for people who "had it made," or who demonstrated that they possessed extraordinary powers. They would have had high praise for any self-help celebrity, or those who brilliantly marketed their own brand of philosophy or religion. They would have appreciated the televangelists, the "megachurches," Scientology, and the worldly success of the Jesus Seminar equally well. But the death of a man on a cross in naked poverty was complete nonsense to them. To them self-emptying humility, whether in Jesus or in Paul his disciple, was neither wise nor strong. It was weak and stupid.

The response of the Apostle Paul is to show that enlightenment is a reversal of all "conventional wisdom" and, in fact, "exposes the pretentious nonsense" of secular power. In spite of its ability to dazzle the intellect, "the world has never had a clue when it comes to knowing God." The wisdom of the cross "is not popular wisdom," he writes, "the fashionable wisdom of high priced experts that will be out of date in a year or so. God's wisdom is something mysterious that goes into the interior of his purpose."[3]

Just as Jesus overturned the tables of the bankers in the temple and drove the buyers and sellers from the House of Prayer, so we must allow Christ crucified to overturn every thought we have of wisdom and to drive out every image of self-embellishing power. The German scholar Hans Conzelmann pointed out that "the summons for the Corinthians to observe themselves is paradoxical in that they are to look where nothing is to be seen."[4] What the world thinks is worthless, useless, and nothing at all, according to Paul in 1 Corinthians 1:26, "is what God has used to destroy what the world considers important." Humility, simplicity, poverty, and self-surrender are in the estimation of our world nothing, but in the end prove to be the only qualities capable of saving us. J. R. R. Tolkien's trilogy *The Lord of the Rings* is a wonderful literary study of a world menaced by hideous evil. In this masterful story it is not someone who is brilliant, tough, famous, or rich, but a simple, good-hearted, trusting little Hobbit who makes his way through many dangers up the mountain of doom to save the world from catastrophic evil. What do you think about that? Do you think that Jesus' crucifixion was a sign of weakness? Or was Jesus' weakness on the cross his strength?

If we look at the cross through the eyes of either irreligion or false religion it appears foolish and weak. The nineteenth-century philosopher Friedrich Nietzsche, for example, found Christianity repugnant because of its morality of love and humility. In

Nietzsche's philosophy whatever enhances self-power is good, and whatever comes from weakness is bad. He had no use for ideals like compassion or self-surrender. In Norman Mailer's novel *The Naked and the Dead*, General Cummings, one of the main characters, whom Nietzsche would have loved, tells his subordinate that "in the future the only morality will be the morality of power."[5] But Cummings, like Nietzsche, is insane, and his morality of power at its best comes to nothing and at its worst ends in senseless death. The viewpoint of Saint Paul is that the weakness of self-emptying love and humility is unimaginably powerful, that self-surrender leads to enlightenment, restores our sanity, and awakens us to real life.

In the early forties Dr. Harry A. Tiebout, a psychiatrist, had among his patients a woman who was a chronic alcoholic. Tiebout's treatment of the woman was totally unsuccessful until he received an early copy of the book *Alcoholics Anonymous* and gave it to her. Tiebout was amazed not only that the woman was able to stay sober, but that as she assimilated the spiritual program of AA the very structure of her character began to change. She became less hostile, less aggressive, and her sense of being out of rhythm with life disappeared. After a vigorous scientific investigation of the personality shift he had witnessed in his patient, Tiebout concluded that two major character flaws plague the alcoholic, which he called *defiant individuality* and *grandiosity*. "Inwardly," Tiebout wrote, "the alcoholic is, and must be master of his or her destiny, and brooks no control from man or God."[6] Tiebout recognized that the reason religion is such a problem for so many alcoholics is that it challenges this tendency to self-deification. But, said Tiebout, if the alcoholic could acknowledge a Higher Power, a Power greater than self, that step alone could bring freedom from the addiction, provided that the step could be taken without resentment.[7] What Tiebout discovered in the laboratory of his clinical practice is a spiritual principle whose antiquity is greater than the universe in which we live. The power of self-surrender is seen precisely in its ability to delivers us from the *blind will* which all the great spiritual traditions of the world have found to be at the root of human bondage. Ask any alcoholic who has discovered sobriety with serenity about the practical wisdom and power of self-surrender.

In the first Corinthian letter it is difficult to separate the qualities of power and wisdom. We have already thought about power. Wisdom, as most simply defined, might be considered the ability to solve complex problems in situations that are filled with uncertainty. It is a particularly insightful and pragmatic way of dealing with serious difficulties. Wisdom involves an intuitive way of knowing. It is an apprehension and appreciation of something apart from logical analysis or sequential reasoning. It is just seeing what is there. More than that, it is seeing the essence of what is there. Most of all, intuitive wisdom involves a kind of understanding that comes more from identifying with something rather than from thinking about it. I want to state quite emphatically that this does not mean that wisdom ever leads to irrational nonsense or lacks intellectual integrity. Wisdom is most certainly not irrational. It is suprarational.

From all this it should be clear that wisdom is not a matter of possessing a piece of information or having high intelligence. Desert wisdom is not so much a quest for philosophical or metaphysical answers to our questions as it is an awakening to the reality of the cross. It is a change in the nature of our awareness. As we experience the truth of the cross we undergo what Scripture calls a *metanoia,* a fundamental shift in the way we think about absolutely everything and every one. Saint James refers to this in his epistle as the "wisdom from above."[8]

James contrasts this spiritual wisdom from above with the

wisdom from below. The wisdom from below is characterized by selfish ambition. It is based on the limits of human thinking and is demonic in its origins. It is demonic because it is murderous, if not physically then emotionally, intellectually, or spiritually. It is a calculus of catastrophe. But divine logic, the spiritual wisdom from above, is characterized by peace, by purity of heart, and by the kind of love that nurtures and enhances life of any kind. It is wisdom in the shape of a cross. The wisdom from below, though initially showing great promise, ends in serious consequences; the wisdom from above, cruciform wisdom, though appearing weak and silly ultimately gets results. A good way of discerning the path we are on is to ask whether the way we are living gets results or consequences.

However, when James says that true wisdom is from above he not only means that its origins are in Divine Mystery, but that wisdom is also a gift from God rather than something we can acquire on our own. James says in the fifth verse of the first chapter of his letter that if we don't know how to make it through the desert, all we have to do is to ask God, the giving God, for wisdom and God will give it. It doesn't matter, James says, whether we have gotten ourselves lost, or whether we are the ones who have created the mess we are in. God will give us the wisdom we need, generously and without criticism. In First Corinthians Paul says very much the same thing. "No one knows the thoughts of God, the deep purposes of God except the Spirit of God," who reveals God's mystery, God's hidden wisdom, "to spiritual people." Enlightenment is a gift the Holy Spirit gives to those who are prepared to receive it. "Every word we speak," writes Paul, "was taught to us by God's Spirit, not by human wisdom. And this same Spirit helps us teach spiritual things to spiritual people."

The words which have been "taught by the Spirit" (1 Cor. 2:13) reveal to us the wisdom of God (1 Cor. 2:7–10), which is

Christ on the cross (1 Cor. 2:8). But only those who have reached a certain level of spiritual maturity can understand these words. This indicates that understanding involves something more than assenting to basic Christian beliefs. It is, unfortunately, obvious to the whole world that even church members may believe in God without worshiping God, that they may live their lives according to the values of a dishonest and cruel culture without ever recognizing the inner contradiction. The unknown writer of the Epistle to the Hebrews reprimands certain believers for their immaturity and urges them to go beyond the elementary teachings of the Christian faith to the deep things of God. In our Corinthian passage Paul identifies two types of individuals who simply cannot understand spiritual wisdom because they are not spiritual. One is the person who attempts to live without faith, without trust in the fundamental goodness of God as seen in Christ. The other is the person who is a Christian believer, but does not live love.

Here is another one of the paradoxes of the Christian faith. On the one hand there is nothing we can do to make ourselves good or wise. Wisdom and holiness are gifts. On the other hand, there is something we can do to receive the gifts of God. Our preparation for enlightenment is not insignificant. The depth of our communion, the extent to which we are transformed by Love, and how much of the incalculable we experience as real is largely up to us. Our encounter with Wisdom, with Mystery, with Christ on the cross, our encounter with the Triune God calls for our participation through prayer, sacred reading, contemplation, and worship.

A careful study of James's use of the word *wisdom* and of Paul's poetic description of love in 1 Corinthians 13 shows the two to be virtually synonymous. The wise person, the enlightened person, the one who knows God is not the woman or man who is capable of great intellectual feats, but rather is the person who loves with a pure heart. Love is itself a way of knowing. There are things about you that no psychiatrist can ever know or understand as well as someone who truly loves you. There are things, deep and hidden and wonderful, about your wife or husband, son or daughter, mother or father, or friend that can only be seen in the light of love. What is true in our relationships with other people is, of course, infinitely more true of our relationship with God. The person who loves deeply is the person who sees deeply, and to whom the true meaning of Scripture is made known.

Through the narrative of the crucifixion the Holy Spirit speaks, like a silent desert breeze, in our hearts—speaks of the hidden purposes of God, and through the "inner eye of love" gives us a vision of God.[9] Through the inspiration of written Scripture as it tells of the passion of Christ, and through the inspiration of our reading the crucifixion story in Scripture, we are enlightened as to God's kindly intention to unite us, to unite everyone, to unite the whole cosmos in love with Christ.

Looking contemplatively at Jesus on the cross we see the limitless love of God that no words or images can describe. The wisdom of the cross becomes our ecstasy. But there is also a profound sorrow in what we see. There is the horror of recognizing that Jesus on the cross is what we do to love. What we discover in the bloody crucifixion of Christ is salvation in the most comprehensive meaning of both the Hebrew and Greek terms—healing, wholeness, preservation of life, rescue from danger, spaciousness, expansiveness, freedom from everything that narrows or constricts life. In the crucifixion we find a forgiveness, a wide mercy, an incomprehensible love, and a wisdom of heart that purifies the poisoned springs of the desert.

In the self-emptying love of Christ, God's innermost nature is revealed. Jesus hanging on the cross is the truest sight of the unseen God we will ever have in this life. Ultimately wisdom is not a foggy idea or a thought or a feeling, but a person. Wisdom is Jesus of Nazareth hanging by the nails in his hands from the crossbeam. Wisdom is Jesus, Son of God, forsaken. We remember this especially at Easter; we remember how he cried out in agony: "My God, my God, why have you forsaken me?" Jesus forsaken shows a love which holds on to nothing, clings to nothing, but instead is willing to lose everything, to let go of everything, to be emptied of everything but love.

The depth of God's love, then, is seen in the pouring out of Christ's life on the cross. The crucifixion of Jesus shows us that the core, the why, of creation is God's love, wisdom, and strength. We become Christian mystics when we see this love, wisdom, and power shining in all things, including our own suffering, and when we understand that cruciform wisdom is something not to be thought but rather to be lived. The call, therefore, to take up our cross every day and follow Jesus can mean nothing less than it meant for Christ to take up his own cross in love for God and for us.

In *A Brief History of Time,* the famous physicist Stephen Hawking says: "We are very close to knowing how the universe was made; but, if we knew why we would know the mind of God."[10] What Saint Paul teaches is that we do know the mind of God, we know why the universe was made, we understand the mystery, not through astrophysics or quantum mechanics, but through cruciform living. "Has anyone ever known," asks Paul, "the thoughts of the Lord or given the Lord advice? But we have the mind of Christ."[11]

Now on that same day two of them were going to a village called Emmaus, about seven miles from Jerusalem, and talking with each other about all these things that had happened. While they were talking and discussing, Jesus himself came near and went with them, but their eyes were kept from recognizing Him. And he said to them, "What are you discussing with each other while you walk along?" They stood still, looking sad....Then he said to them, "Oh, how foolish you are, and how slow of heart to believe all that the prophets have declared!"... Then beginning with Moses and all the prophets, he interpreted to them the things about himself in all the scriptures.

As they came near to the village to which they were going, he walked ahead as if he were going on. But they urged him strongly, saying, "Stay with us because it is almost evening and the day is now nearly over." So he went in to stay with them. When he was at the table with them, he took bread, blessed and broke it, and gave it to them. Then their eyes were opened, and they recognized him; and he vanished from their sight. They said to each other, "Were not our hearts burning within us while he was talking to us on the road, while he was opening the scriptures to us?"

That same hour they got up and returned to Jerusalem; and they found the eleven and their companions gathered together.... Then they told what had happened on the road, and how he had been made known to them in the breaking of the bread.

Luke 24:13–35 (NRSV)

VII

A Vision of the Moon

Christ is the moon because the people who wrote the Gospel are leading their readers to a vision not only of the historical Jesus (of whom we assuredly can have concepts) but of the risen Christ, the cosmic Christ, the Christ who was at the beginning. And it is he who escapes all images, all thoughts, all ideas, and all pictures. The risen Christ is so far beyond all concepts that we find Paul struggling with all kinds of words to express the inexpressible.... For Paul Christ is a "secret" or a "mystery" or whatever you want to call it, and Paul keeps pointing one finger after another at the moon that no human eye can descry. The poor scholars get all tied up in Paul's fingers; the mystics turn toward the moon.

William Johnston, SJ, *Lord Teach Us To Pray*

In *My Quest for Beauty*, Rollo May tells of a profound Easter experience on Mount Athos.[1] The little Byzantine church at the monastery of Stavronikita was filled with incense, and hundreds of flickering candles gave a mystical aura to the whole sanctuary. The service lasted all through the night. At its conclusion, early in the morning, the monks with all the people passed before the abbot who greeted each one with the words *"Christos Anesti!"* — meaning "Christ is risen!" To which each person responded, according to the custom, *"Alethos Anesti!"* — "Truly He has risen!" May writes: "I was seized by a moment of spiritual reality: what would it mean to our world if He had truly risen?" Yes! What does it mean if Christ is truly risen?

To Cleopas and his friend on the road to Emmaus that Sunday morning, it meant hope, it meant "What no eye has seen, nor ear heard, nor the human heart conceived, what God has prepared for those who love him" (1 Cor. 2:9 NRSV). Apparently they had been with the eleven and the others earlier in the morning and had heard the women's report that the tomb was empty, but this did not suggest to them that Jesus was now the risen Lord; in fact, they seemed to have thought that the story was some sort of "hysterical craziness." It was with heavy hearts and sad faces that they walked the road toward the village of Emmaus. And as they walked they thought about and spoke of all the things that had happened concerning "Jesus of Nazareth, who was a prophet mighty in deed and word before God and all the people" (Luke 24:19 NRSV); they talked about Jesus' sentence to death, and the horrible crucifixion. Three days had passed and the awful finality of his death had begun to sink in, so that not even the reports of an empty tomb could stir any hope.

The death of Jesus had left these two travelers with an acute awareness of the transitoriness of life, of their human finitude, of their—and seemingly Christ's—inability to keep something good from coming to nothing. Jesus' death left them adrift on a sea of uncertainty, confusion, and despair. It overwhelmed them with a sense of the utter contingency of life. If you have been through the death of someone you love very much, you probably know how those closest to Jesus felt. His death meant the crumbling of their whole world, of their whole life. The tortured death of Christ utterly destroyed the meaning and joy they had just found in following him. In their sorrow the two disciples on the road to Emmaus may even have felt somewhat like the cynical F. Scott Fitzgerald, who said, "Life is a cheat, and its chief condition is despair." Is the chief condition of life despair? Is goodness ultimately impotent in the face of evil? Are all thoughts of a higher, more satisfying life beyond death nothing more than a silly denial of our mortality? Do love and kindness and compassion and honesty finally come to absolutely nothing? What will it mean if we succeed in eliminating the capricious and copious violence of a bloody and brutal world, or the unnecessary suffering of the poor, if it all ends in the fiery collapse of the solar system? When asked to speak to the people, the prophet said (and I am paraphrasing here): "No! Why should I? They are just grass."[2] The prophet seems to be asking, What is the point of trying to do anything, if like the new tender grass the people will all soon be dead? What, we may ask, if the atheistic existentialists are right? What if there is no wise and loving Presence? What if life is completely absurd—without significance or meaning of any kind? That is despair.

Because it is a journey through despair, the walk to Emmaus is a desert journey. This is a wilderness testing that Cleopas and the other disciple go through. But precisely because the sorrowful sense of the impermanence of the universe is a desert experience, it can lead to purification of heart as we let go, one by one, of all our hopes until we are left with hope in God alone. This is what T. S. Eliot was getting at in his poetry when he wrote: "Wait without hope, for hope would be hope for the wrong thing."[3] All our hopes and dreams must be shattered, must die, so that only the one hope remains—"the mystery of the ages which is Christ in you, the hope of glory" (Col. 1:27). Glory is the shining of God's presence in love. Resurrection hope is the hope of knowing the mystery of Christ's unending presence.

The two despairing travelers meet Jesus on the road, but there is no recognition or awareness of who is present with them. Jesus' identity remains hidden to them, as it always remains hidden to those who have not been initiated into the mysteries of the faith. Jesus' response is direct, "Oh, how foolish you are, and how slow of heart to believe all that the prophets have declared!"[4] It seems unreasonable to them to think that the one who had suffered and died could be the promised Lord of Glory. "They just cannot see," as Amy Grant sang in "El Shadda," how God's "most awesome work was done through the frailty of the Son." But what is it that makes us so slow of heart to believe? With his usual perceptiveness Thomas Merton saw how much we are like the women who went to the tomb early Easter morning to embalm the body of Jesus. Their great worry was how to move the massive stone from the entrance to the sepulcher so that they could get to the lifeless body. In *He Is Risen*, Merton wrote, "Though we may still say with our lips that Christ is risen we secretly believe him in practice to be dead. And we believe that there is a massive stone blocking the way and keeping us from getting to his dead body. This is the result of substituting something else for the Living Presence and Light of Christ in our lives."[5] For some people the "something else" that becomes a massive stone keeping them from "the Living Presence and Light of Christ" is a problem not of the intellect but of the will. Consciously there is some great intellectual problem that prevents them from abandoning themselves to the gratuitous love of the risen Christ, but unconsciously they are terrified by the thought of self-surrender. For others, the immovable stone is a substitution of either overbelief or underbelief for the mystical presence of Christ.

Overbelief tends toward legalism and religion by formula.

Its understanding of the Christian faith usually has a highly forensic quality to it; that is, its thinking is like courtroom thinking. It approaches spiritual matters in much the same way that an attorney or judge might approach a legal case. Or the Bible is regarded as a question-and-answer book so that the reading of Scripture is rather flat and one-dimensional. As it gets expressed in Christian worship and in personal life, overbelief tends to make small what is large. It is simply too trivial to be true.

Underbelief tends to read into Scripture what it would like to find there, and to read out of the Bible what it does not want to find. Underbelief frequently attempts to distinguish between the Jesus of history and the Christ of faith, but its methodology for determining the authenticity of what Jesus said and did is simply too scientifically flawed to be of any real use. The Jesuit scholar and contemplative William Johnston makes this pertinent comment: "If one has a minimum of fidelity to Paul and John and Luke, and the rest, one sees that the cosmic Christ is precisely the Jesus who shed his blood."[6] The Jesus that underbelief presents to us is a heck of a nice guy, probably an aware social activist, and dispenses some really good self-help tips. But none of this is sufficient to account for the breath-taking impact Jesus has had on our world. Nor can it account for Christ's continuing power to so dramatically transform the lives of individual men and women. The only thing significant about the Jesus of underbelief is the wild and false rumors started by his followers. The truth is there is not much about the Jesus of underbelief that really matters. In the end the banality of underbelief renders it implausible and humdrum.

Both underbelief and overbelief are obsessed with convincing people through syllogistic reasoning to assent to certain theories. Both perceive the biblical text as an object to be controlled and mastered by their cognitive powers. Neither has the capacity to let a text speak for itself. Neither is willing to seek the desert where the whisper and the thunder of God can be heard in contemplative listening. We could say with Merton that the real problem is not the stone in front of the tomb. The tomb is empty. Jesus is risen! Nothing is a substitute for the "Living Presence and Light of Christ in our lives."

Jesus listened to the two disciples share their sorrow, their feelings of hopelessness and emptiness. "Then beginning with Moses and all the prophets, he interpreted to them the things about himself in all the scriptures."[7] This unpretentious sentence says something truly astounding about Christian spirituality. What it says is that Scripture reveals the secret of who Jesus is.

All Scripture points to Jesus Christ as the suffering servant who is now the glorified Lord—the Cosmic Christ. In his confrontation with the clergy and religion scholars Jesus says, "You diligently study the Scriptures because you think that by them you possess eternal life. These are the Scriptures that testify about me, yet you refuse to come to me to have life."[8] The word *study* in this verse does not suggest spiritual insight but meticulous analysis. These are religious people who really want to know the Scriptures, but the true method of knowing Scripture is by *agape*—unrestrained personal commitment which renounces all selfish striving. Understanding Scripture comes in two ways: one is from a purely academic study, the other from knowing the Lord Himself. The one is abstract, rationalistic, and detached from life. The other is a loving response to God's grace so that what we read and study is inseparable from our experience of Christ. To quote Nee To-sheng's *What Shall This Man Do?*: "First comes trouble, desperation, experience—and life; then afterwards doctrine. It is not in searching, studying, comparing, but at the place of desperation that God gives life."[9] Scripture discloses the true identity of Christ, and when we are able to absorb Scripture like the desert sand absorbs a drop of rain, then we will know Christ.

What we discover, in Luke's description of Jesus' opening the Scriptures on the walk to Emmaus, is that Christ is present wherever Scripture is read and heard. Cleopas and his friend later ask each other, "Were not our hearts burning within us while he was talking with us on the road, while he was opening the scriptures to us?"[10] Central to Christian spirituality is the knowledge that Christ is present in his word, and joins with us in every sincere and honest conversation concerning his word, just as he was a participant in the Emmaus Road conversation.

As Jesus shares the mysteries of Scripture with the two disciples there is a growing feeling that they are of one heart; a warm sense of closeness develops between the three of them. Although the two disciples do not yet fully recognize who it is that is present with them, the stranger is no longer really a stranger, but a friend. So as they finally reach their house in the village, and it looks as if their traveling companion is set to go his own way, they invite him to come in and to stay the night with them. Now if Cleopas is another form of the name Clopas, who is mentioned as the husband of Mary in John 19:25, then the story becomes especially poignant as Mary and Cleopas invite the unrecognized Christ into their home. Home is that place where we truly belong. It is where we are the most easily and naturally our true selves. Henri Nouwen said in *With Burning Hearts*, "One of the most decisive moments of the Eucharist—and of our life—is the moment of invitation. Do we say: 'It was wonderful to meet you, thank you for your insights, your advice, and your encouragement. I hope the rest of your journey goes well. Goodbye!' Or do we say: 'I have heard you. My heart is changing . . . please come into my home and see where and how I live!'"[11] This invitation to come in and to spend the evening in their home means that Mary and Cleopas want Jesus to be more to them than a stimulating conversationalist or a fascinating character they happened to meet on the road. Their invitation means that they do not want to keep their distance from him, they don't want him to remain a stranger; they want to become the closest of friends with him. Jesus accepts the invitation, and as they begin to eat their evening meal something new and lovely begins to happen, a wonderful reversal takes place. The stranger, as Nouwen points out, becomes the gracious host. "He who was invited now invites. The two disciples who trusted the stranger enough to let him enter their inner space are now led into the inner life of their host."[12]

"After Jesus sat down to eat, he took some bread. He blessed it and broke it. Then he gave it to them. At once they knew who he was, but he disappeared."[13] Here Luke is clearly picturing the celebration of the Lord's Supper, the eucharistic worship of the earliest church. All of the elements are there: take, bless, break, and give. The meal at Emmaus in which Christ makes himself known is therefore to be identified with the supper on the night before he died and with the eucharistic meal of the earliest Christians at worship.

As the bread is taken, blessed, broken, and given they suddenly recognize that it is Jesus who is present with them. They understand now the connection between the crucified Christ and the Risen Lord of Glory. This wonderful and artistically told story, which climaxes in the Lord's Supper, climaxes in what can only be understood as eucharistic worship. It is a story of mystical communion. It is the story of the human yearning to belong to God, and of God's eternal desire to embrace the whole world in an intimate union of love. It is a story of what happens when both Creator and creature join in self-emptying love. It is a story that becomes deeper and more real every time bread is taken, blessed, broken, and given. Every time we drink from the cup of blessing with happy and open hearts, the presence of Christ becomes more literal. Henri Nouwen articulated it so beautifully:

In the Eucharist Jesus gives all. The bread is not just a sign of his desire to become our food; the cup is not just a sign of his willingness to be our drink. Bread and wine *become* his body and blood in the giving. The bread indeed is his body given for us; the wine his blood poured out for us. As God becomes fully present for us in Jesus, so Jesus becomes fully present to us in the bread and wine of the Eucharist. God not only became flesh for us years ago in a country far away. God also becomes food and drink for us now at the moment of the Eucharistic celebration, right where we are together around the table. God does not hold back; God gives all. That is the mystery of the Incarnation. That too is the mystery of the Eucharist. Incarnation and Eucharist are the two expressions of the immense, self-giving love of God. And so the sacrifice on the cross and the sacrifice at the table are one sacrifice, one complete, divine self-giving that reaches out to all humanity in time and space. The word that best expresses this mystery of God's total self-giving love is "communion." It is the word that contains the truth that, in and through Jesus, God wants, not only to teach us, instruct us, or inspire us, but to become one with us.[14]

But as they experienced this moment of perfect clarity, of Perfect Presence in the breaking of bread, Christ disappeared. The miraculous disappearance points to the way in which the presence of Christ the Lord is now to be known. Christ is known where Scripture is read, prayed, meditated, contemplated. And we see Christ as real and present, as the one who is our constant companion on all of life's roads, as we eat the bread and drink the cup at the Lord's Table. Once the disciples have recognized Jesus as the risen Lord, his bodily presence is no longer required as a condition of faith and hope. They now have an unshakable certainty in a literal relationship of love with the resurrected Cosmic Christ.

At this point I must say, quite emphatically, that the resurrection of Jesus is not merely a demonstration of the power of God or of the uniqueness of Jesus Christ. Rather, it is the picturing of the *Christus Victor* understanding of Jesus' resurrection in which the power of evil, cruelty, and death are overcome. Furthermore, Christ's triumphant resurrection is also the means by which resurrection life is extended to all humanity, so that by dying Jesus opens the way to eternal life—to that large and perpetual life, to that spaciousness and total freedom which is meant by salvation.

Prior to modern physics the whole idea of resurrection was probably more difficult to accept than it is now. The Anglican priest and former Cambridge professor of mathematics John Polkinghorne observes that what is important are not the specific atoms that presently constitute my body, but the pattern of atoms. It is therefore reasonable to believe that God re-created the pattern of Jesus, and to hope that by God's "great act of final resurrection" God will re-create the pattern that is the real me.[15] Charles Perry, in *The Resurrection Promise,* prefers to use the word *re-creation* rather than *resurrection.* Perry writes, "Resurrection refers obviously to a transformation or metamorphosis of Jesus, effected by God, from an earthly and perishable body to what Paul refers to as a 'spiritual body.' The first died on the cross, and the second is a new creation. The two are related in that the spiritual body of the Risen One can be identified with Jesus of Nazareth, who was crucified."[16] C. W. McPherson in *Understanding Faith* states what is central to Christian thought: "Many cults assert that while their leader's body is destroyed, 'his soul goes marching on.' Christianity asserts the resurrection, the full, complete rising to life of Jesus, body and soul. The Greek word is *anastasis,* a wonderfully simple word picture meaning roughly 'standing there all over again.'"[17] If Jesus was not "standing there all over again" on the road to Emmaus, if Christ was not resurrected, if Christ is alive only metaphorically and not in very fact, then there is no mystical experience of Christ's presence. The Jesuit scholar Gerald O'Collins points out that the resurrection may be "underinterpreted" to mean that the disciples "found value in Jesus' message and example," but not that there was a "full and complete" rising of Jesus on Easter morning.[18] O'Collins asserts that underinterpreting the biblical narratives to be merely symbolic affirmations of some general principle such as love runs counter to all the evidence. Underinterpretation may make the Emmaus narrative more acceptable to a skeptical world, but if after Good Friday Jesus' body disintegrated in a grave somewhere in ancient Palestine then Christ may be present as a fond and inspiring memory but not in fact.[19]

The disappearance of Jesus as he sat at the table that evening in Emmaus says that Jesus is now the Cosmic Christ, beyond all images, thoughts, formulas and concepts. The same Jesus who suffered and died is the Lord of Glory who dwells in that mysterious place beyond all time and place, and who makes his home in the depths of a humble, emptied heart. John, the beloved disciple, said: "We have seen the glory of Christ."[20] For Saint John, as with Saint Paul, Christ is "the primacy over all created things" and "holds all things in unity."[21] In John's Gospel Christ is "the true vine, the true way, the true life, the true truth."[22] The Gospel of John sums up the cosmic dimensions of Christ in the cryptic saying of Jesus: "And I, when I am lifted up from the earth, I will draw all people to myself."[23]

Go out past the farthest city lights; go well beyond the artificial glow that distorts and makes it impossible to see the stunning beauty of the heavens at night. Go far out into the desert where the darkness is clean and clear. And look up at the moon so large you feel like you can touch it, its familiar face so distinct. Look up at the moon which bathes the quiet desert with its gentle light. Look up at the moon and wonder. Look up at the moon and sing alleluia, alleluia!

Appendices

Appendix A
About Small Groups

Alleluia Is the Song of the Desert is intended for use by small groups. By participating together in a Lenten group, or in a small group for spiritual formation, we can become somewhat like a monastic desert community whose members support one another in seeking spiritual direction and in growing toward a more intimate and contemplative experience of God's presence.

A number of group formats are possible:

1. A group could simply come together each week as an informal discussion group and talk about the material and the questions in each chapter. In that case I suggest that the discussion center on what has come up for people personally in reading the chapter for the week rather than revolving around abstract ideas.

2. A meeting could be structured so as to begin with a brief prayer, followed by thirty minutes of sharing of what is happening in members' lives, then forty-five minutes discussing the questions in the text, and finally fifteen minutes of praying conversationally with one another.

3. A third option is to use the small group exercises in Appendix C. These exercises are given in some detail, and are even scripted

in places. They are experiential in their orientation, with the corresponding book chapters furnishing the context rather than being the focal point of the exercises.

4. A larger number of people might meet as a single group, have someone give a short lecture or lead a discussion based on the book, and then divide into small groups to do the exercises.

If you are organizing a small group, make sure that everyone you invite clearly understands the purpose, content, and process of the group. Let people know the time and place of meetings, and who will be leading or facilitating the group. People will want to know how long each session will last; there is enough material for one to two hours, depending on your preference. Whatever you decide, be clear about the length of the meeting and remember that it is important to begin and end on time. The people you invite to participate in the group should be people who want to come in order to deepen their relationship with God rather than to acquire more information in a study session. They should be people who do not need to take charge of every group they are in, but who can both give and receive in a group meeting. It is probably best not to encourage people who cannot attend every time since this will interfere with developing the trust among members that is so important to the process.

If you are not going to lead the group yourself then you will need to find a facilitator. If you are the facilitator, your job is to lead the exercises, to watch the time according to the agenda, and to moderate any discussion, making sure that discussion and sharing stays focused on the content, atmosphere, and attitudes that form the group's reason for being. As the facilitator you will need to arrange for necessary handouts, like the Guidelines for Small Groups (Appendix B); or music, and any needed equipment, decorations, or religious symbols; and for the participation of other people in reading and praying. In writing the exercises, I frequently relied on several books: *Gathered in the Word* by Norvene Vest,[1] *Surrender: A Guide for Prayer* by Jacqueline Syrup Bergan and S. Marie Schwan,[2] and *Too Deep for Words* by Thelma Hall.[3] You may find it helpful to consult these books along with Rose Mary Dougherty's *Group Spiritual Direction.*[4]

As Dougherty notes, in advocating a contemplative group atmosphere: "If group members are going to help one another be attentive to God, they need to try to be attentive to God during the meetings themselves."[5] Meetings need to be held in a way and in a place that encourages openness, calmness, and attentiveness to the holy. At one time I encouraged small groups to meet in someone's living room, but the comfortable sofas and overstuffed chairs in a living room often make it difficult for people to become spiritually centered or attentive to the presence of God. They are more likely to sit back, prop up their feet, and shoot the breeze. Chairs should be comfortable, but with straight backs and arranged in a circle. If you are not meeting in someplace like a church, then think about how you can decorate the room easily in a way that gives a sense of its being a sacred place. Lighting should be subdued, just bright enough to read by. You might be able to get by with candlelight. I would suggest having an unscented candle on a table in the center. Don't fumble around with any equipment like CD players, and don't engage in little side conversations when you are making a transition, for example, when you are about to sing. All of that is a distraction and ruins the atmosphere.

> Every once in a while we meet (perhaps are given by God) another person or a group of kindred spirits where for a brief period of time we have a glimpse into the way things could be, the community to which we really are called. In that setting our de-

91

sire for God comes alive, and we feel supported in our desire by the person or the group. Even though we might never see them again, we know that there is something we've "touched into" together. The essence of what we have "touched into" continues to be with us, nurturing our desire long after we have separated.[6]

Appendix B
Guidelines for Small Groups

It is essential
1. To maintain strict confidentiality. Do not tell others what you hear or what happens in the group.
2. Not to give advice or to offer solutions for someone else's problem.
3. Not to moralize, judge, preach, correct, or criticize.
4. Not to minimize or make light of what anyone says.
5. Not to catastrophize or exaggerate the significance of what someone says.
6. That we make this group a safe place where people are free to feel and say what is in their hearts.

You are encouraged
1. To refrain from any cross-talk or side conversations.
2. To help in creating an atmosphere of attentive listening and reverence.
3. To share honestly from your heart.
4. To stay focused on spiritual issues rather than getting involved in intellectual discussions or derailed by unrelated topics.
5. To listen to the facilitator for clues as to how much time it is appropriate to take in sharing.

You may choose not to share
1. Any time you do not want to share, just say, "I pass."
2. It is unlikely that you will feel uncomfortable with any of the exercises, but if you do, you need not participate. Just sit quietly and prayerfully until it is over.

It is appropriate to share
1. How you feel about what is happening in your life right now.
2. Decisions you are facing, or the direction in which you sense God leading you at this time.
3. Your own spiritual issues and questions of character raised by what is happening at work, in your family, or in other relationships.
4. What your prayer life is like and what you experience in prayer—joy or sadness, peace or anxiety, love or anger.
5. Your spiritual or religious experiences.
6. How you experience God—close or distant, caring or indifferent, mysterious.

Appendix C
Spiritual Exercises for Small Groups

First Meeting—Week of One Lent
INTO THE DESERT

1. Opening

- You might begin by lighting a candle, singing or listening to a Taizé song or some other meditative piece of music, or sitting in silence.
- Read the narrative of Jesus' baptism and desert testing from Mark 1:9–13.
- Pray, expressing our desire for God, and asking God to make God's presence known to us in the forty days of our Lenten Desert.
- State the parameters of the group.

a. Concerning why we are here. The basic assumption which guides us is that we are here because of our desire for God, and because we believe that in a small group like this we can find support for our faith and strengthen our spiritual practice.

b. Concerning responsibility to one another. Have copies of "Guidelines for Small Groups" (Appendix B) to hand out. For the sake of brevity read the guidelines without a lot of explaining.

c. Concerning the use of silence. You might note that silence is an important part of our group experience, that silence is a way of making space for God, and that it is a way of our entering the desert together. We will usually have at least one minute of silence at the beginning, but by the last meeting we will practice ten minutes of silence in centering prayer.

d. Concerning the role of the facilitator. Emphasize that your job is to facilitate the meeting by getting the meeting started, by keeping things on track, and by intervening if the group has been deflected from its purpose.

2. Getting Acquainted

• The following questions will help members of the group both to get acquainted and to focus on their relationship with God. (An asterisk indicates words that are to be said aloud by the facilitator.)

a. * I want to ask you four sets of questions that will help us to get to know one another better. We will need to keep our answers fairly brief so that we can get through everything we have planned. I will answer each question first, and then we will go around the circle. The first set of questions is (1) What is your name? (2) Where did you live between the ages of eight and twelve? (3) And how many brothers and sisters did you have at the time? [If you are the facilitator, answer the question *briefly* yourself first and then go around the group.]

b. *The second question is: How did you heat your home at that time? [Mention anything unusual or humorous about the heating in your home at that time.]

c. *The third question is: Where was the center of human warmth in your home? It may have been a person, a place, or an activity; or for some of you there may have been no center of human warmth.

d. *The fourth question is: When, if ever, did God become more than a word for you?

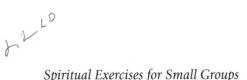
3. An Exercise of Quiet Desire

- *Please listen thoughtfully to this excerpt from *The Awakened Heart* by Gerald May.

There is a desire within each of us, in the deep center of ourselves that we call our heart. We were born with it, it is never completely satisfied, and it never dies. We are often unaware of it, but it is always awake. It is the human desire for love. Every person on earth yearns to love, to be loved, to know love. Our true identity, our reason for being, is to be found in this desire. . . . You can find evidence of this longing in great art, music, literature, and religions; a common universal passion for love runs through them all. . . . But for real proof you must look at your own longings and aspirations; you must listen to the deep themes of your own life story. In most of us the desire for love has often been distorted or buried, but if you look at your own life with honest and gentle eyes, you can discern it in yourself as a deep seeking for connectedness, healing, creation and joy. . . . You probably already know your longing very well. You have felt it as hope for relationship, meaning, fulfillment, perhaps even a sense of destiny. . . . Remember some moment in your life when you felt complete and fulfilled; what did you taste there? Recall also feeling bad, alone, worthless; what were you missing? If you pause and look quietly inside, you may be able to sense something of your desire for love (for God) right now in this moment. Sometimes it is wonderful to touch this deep longing: It can seem expansive and joyful. At other times it can be painful, lonely, and even a little frightening. Whether it feels good or bad, its power and depth are awesome. . . . It is possible to run away from the desire for years, even decades at a time, but we cannot eradicate it entirely. It keeps touching us in little glimpses and hints in our dreams, our hopes, and our unguarded moments. We may go to sleep, but our desire for love (for God) does not. It is who we are. Sometimes in moments of quiet wonder, it is possible to simply be there with our desire.[1]

- Invitation to silent prayer.

    *So now I invite you to settle into a comfortable position with your back straight and eyes closed, and we will take five minutes for silent prayer.

*Scan your body from head to toe and relax any areas of tension you find. Take a slow deep breath and hold it to the count of four and then exhale slowly. [Facilitator counts out loud.] Let your breathing become slow, deep, and regular. Let any distracting thought float away like a helium-filled balloon. Don't try to make anything happen. Don't try to keep anything from happening. Relax into God's loving care. Allow yourself to be deeply relaxed while staying alert and awake. Relaxed and awake. Relaxed and awake. Insofar as it is possible, simply rest in God's presence. In the stillness, you may have a sense of what it is you really want—of the deepest desire within you rising to the surface. Don't try to define it or analyze it. Just let it be. Sit with it in simple and grateful awareness.

3. Discussion

• As time permits, discuss:

a. What, if anything, happened in the silence? Were you able to enter the desert place? What emerged for you out of the stillness? Would anyone like to share?

b. After reading the first chapter, how do you understand sin and repentance? In what ways does this represent a change in or difference to your understanding?

c. Where or how have you been most aware of experiencing the desire for self-surrender—the desire for God?

d. Where do you most feel the forces at work that seek to prevent or undermine your sense of surrender and willingness?

4. Close

• You may want to close by standing, joining hands in a circle, and praying the Lord's Prayer together.

Second Meeting—Week of Two Lent
ALLELUIA IS THE SONG

1.Opening

- Begin with singing and candle lighting.
- Say: *Long ago a great rabbi said, "When you pray know before whom you stand." We are going to observe a minute of silence now in order to become God-focused, and as an indication of our desire to enter into "desert consciousness."
- Conclude with a short verbal prayer expressing the group's desire for God's presence and the group's intention of being present to God in the Lenten Desert.
- Remind members of their responsibilities to one another and to the group (Appendix B).

2. Group *Lectio Divina:* Praying Luke 4:1–13

- Instructions/script
a. *We are going to use a group form of the ancient discipline of *lectio divina,* or sacred reading, which is simply a way of reflecting deeply on Scripture and of making Scripture-reading a prayer. The passage we are going to pray is Jesus' temptation in the desert, found here in Luke 4:1–13.
b. *Prepare for the reading by sitting with feet flat on the floor, back straight, and becoming both relaxed and alert. Close your eyes, take a deep breath, hold it—and then sigh it all out. Breathe deeply, slowly, regularly.
c. *I will read the passage twice, and as I do listen for the word or phrase to which you feel particularly drawn.
d. After having read the passage twice, instruct the group to silently reflect on the passage for one minute, and see what word or phrase attracts them.
e. Silence.

f. *Let's go around the circle now and you can share the word or phrase you were drawn to, but don't elaborate. Just share your word or phrase. [Facilitator may share first.]

g. *Now close your eyes and become centered and listen as the passage is read again, this time by N [ask another member of the group to read this time], and is followed by a few minutes of silence for reflection, asking yourself: "How is my life touched today?"

h. Reading of Luke 4:1–13

i. A few minutes of silence.

j. *I invite any of you, to share how you sense your life being touched by this passage.

k. *In re-reading the passage, keep in mind the question, "Is there some request of me in this passage? Is it calling me to do or to be something?" You will have five minutes of silence to reflect on this question at the end of the reading.

l. Ask someone else to read Luke 4:1–13 a final time.

m. Five minutes of silence.

n. After the silence: *Would anyone like to share, perhaps at a little greater length, something you feel called or drawn to do or be by this passage?

3. Discussion

• As time permits, discuss: Is there something in the first two chapters of the book, or in a worship service since Ash Wednesday, that has affected you personally? (Try to avoid a discussion of ideas, and stay focused on what is happening in people's hearts.)

4. Close

• Stand, join hands, and pray the Lord's Prayer in unison.

Third Meeting—Week of Three Lent
THE CONJURER

1. Opening
- Begin with singing and candle lighting.
- Frederick W. Faber wrote these lines of poetry:

  Only to sit and think of God.
  Oh what a joy it is!
  To think the thought, to breathe the Name
  Earth has no higher bliss.[2]

  Take a moment of silence in which to sit and breathe the Name.
- Say a brief prayer expressing your desire to be with God during this time.
- If helpful, remind members of their responsibilities to one another and to the group (Appendix B).

2. Examen of Consciousness:
- Explanation. *This time together will be focused on the discipline of the examen of consciousness. In an examen of consciousness, we attempt to discover how God has been present to us in our daily lives, and how we have responded to that presence.
- The Exercise

a. *Settle into a comfortable position with your feet on the floor, your back straight, and your eyes closed. Take a deep breath and hold it to the count of four. [Facilitator counts out loud.] Now exhale slowly like a great sigh. Take another deep breath, hold it to the count of four, and sigh it all out. Scan your body and relax any areas of tension you find. Let your breathing become deep, slow, and regular. Deep, slow, and regular. Let all distractions float away. Allow yourself to become deeply relaxed while remaining awake to everything. As I pray out loud, you may pray silently with me. When I pause, silently give your own personal response as it emerges within you.

    Facilitator: *God, I am totally and completely dependent on You. It is in You "that I live, move, and have my very being." Your Spirit is my *Breath.* All of life is a gift from you. I give you thanks and praise for the good things of this day. [pause]

b. *Facilitator continuing:* *You have been present in my heart and Your Spirit is at work in my life today. Be with me now as I consider Your presence and work. I see Your presence in the feelings I have experienced [pause] . . . In the events of today [pause] . . . In your call to me [pause] . . . And in the people and events of today [pause] . . . I sense Your presence in the way I have responded to You [pause] . . .

    O God, I ask for Your forgiveness and healing. The particular event of this day I most want forgiven or healed is [pause] . . .

    Filled with hope and faith in Your inexhaustible love and power, I entrust myself to Your care. Amen.

3. Discussion

- Use any or all of the following suggestions for discussion:

a. Would any of you like to share what happened within you in this examen of consciousness?

b. During the last week, in what ways have you experienced God's presence, or your desire for God?

c. In reading this last chapter, "The Conjurer," have you become aware of any ways in which you have been "conjured"? How about your use of power?

d. How do you feel about allowing answers to emerge from within you and waiting for the moment of right action, rather than trying to "make things happen"?

4. Close

- Stand in a circle, join hands, and repeat the Lord's Prayer in unison.

Fourth Meeting—Week of Four Lent
THE THIRD TEST

1. Opening
- Begin with singing and candle lighting.
- Read the following excerpt from Henri J. M. Nouwen's *The Way of the Heart.*

> Arsenius was a well-educated Roman of senatorial rank who lived at the court of Emperor Theodosius as tutor to the princes Arcadius and Honorisus. While still living in the palace, Abba Arsenius prayed to God in these words, "Lord lead me in the way of salvation." And a voice came saying to him, "Arsenius, flee from the world and you will be saved." Having sailed secretly from Rome to Alexandria and having withdrawn to the solitary life (in the desert) Arsenius prayed again: "Lord lead me in the way of salvation." And again he heard a voice saying, "Arsenius, *flee, be silent,* and *pray* always, for these are the sources of sinlessness." The words flee, be silent and pray summarize the spirituality of the desert. They indicate the three ways of preventing the world from shaping us in its image and are thus the three ways to life in the Spirit.[3]

- *So let's observe one minute of silent prayer as a way of welcoming God and entering the desert. After a minute of silent prayer I [facilitator] will conclude with a verbal prayer.
- Facilitator says a brief prayer welcoming God and expressing gratitude for this time of turning to God.
- If helpful, remind members of their responsibilities to one another and to the group (Appendix B).

2. Read Luke 4: 9–13

3. *Lectio* on Life: Praying Your Life
- Instructions/script
- a. *Earlier we used a spiritual practice known as *lectio divina*, which

is a way of praying Scripture. We used it as way of praying Luke 4:1–13. Now we are going to use a modern exercise known as "*lectio* on life." You can think of it as a way of praying your life.

b. *To begin, sit in a relaxed and comfortable position: feet flat on the floor, back straight, eyes closed. Take a deep breath and hold it to the count of four. [Repeat three times.] Scan your body from head to toe and from toe to head for any tense muscles. Gently relax any muscular tension in your body. Let go of all preoccupations and troubling thoughts. Become completely centered in the present moment. If a thought or image comes floating down the stream of consciousness, just let it float by. Become completely relaxed. Relaxed and awake.

c. *Begin very gently, and with some objective detachment, as if you were watching a video, to mentally review the events of the last few hours, days, or week. The idea is to recall your recent experiences, hour by hour and day by day. As each memory passes by, you may begin to notice one that recurs, or that feels more important than the others. Use the next five minutes of silence to choose one particular event and hold it gently and easily in your mind.

d. Five minutes of silence.

e. *When you are ready, you can open your eyes. I have a simple question for you. Approximately what time of day was it when the incident you chose occurred? [Go around the circle.]

f. *We will try to explore now how our lives have been touched by God in Christ through our experience. Let me remind you that you will not have to share anything you don't care to, but you may still find doing the exercise helpful.

g. *Get comfortable. Close your eyes and take one minute to review the event again. Note any physical aspect to the experience like colors, shapes, sounds, smells, or textures. Keeping your eyes closed, recall the event emotionally. Where in your incident did you experience the strongest emotion, positive or negative? Were there any points at which your emotions shifted? Take one minute of silence for this task.

h. *[After a minute of silence for the above, take two minutes for the following]: *With eyes still closed, set this specific event aside. In so far as possible, let go of all thoughts and feelings. Let them all float away. Just be in the empty expanse of the desert. With a free and open mind see if there is not some phrase or image that now seems to surface for you. It may be a phrase from Scripture, a song, or a story. Don't worry about where the image or phrase comes from, or the logical fit, just let it come. Perhaps in your image or phrase you will receive some sort of a blessing, or see how Christ was present in the incident.

i. *Maybe in just a sentence or two you would be willing to share the phrase or image of blessing you discovered. Not the event itself, just the phrase or image of blessing. It is, of course, all right if you choose to pass. Let's go around the circle.

j. *Close your eyes again. Remember that Christ is here with us. Relax, and rest in his presence. Bring back into your mind both the experience you remembered and the phrase or image associated with it. Picture yourself approaching an altar to God, and on the altar you place both the incident and the phrase or image of blessing you were given. Everything associated with the incident, all the feelings, the incident itself, the blessing are placed on the altar with your phrase or image on top. Everything—any pain, confusion, insight, thoughts, blessing—is offered back to God. We will have about a minute of silence to complete our offerings.

k. *Keeping your eyes closed, reflect on your experience. Does there seem to be an invitation or a call in it? Perhaps as you were making your offering to God you had an insight. Or it may be that now your feelings about it have completely changed. The invitation may be in your word or phrase. Take a moment to silently reflect on whether you are being called to do or be something in the immediate future.

l. *I invite each of you to share what happened in you, if you wish. How has Christ touched your heart in this time of reflection?

3. Discussion

• As time permits, discuss:

a. Do you identify with Bonhoeffer's poem "Who Am I?" If so, in what ways? Have you been able to reach the same sort of resolution as Bonhoeffer?

b. Would you care to share a time when you have asked the question: "Is God here or not?"

c. Read and discuss 2 Corinthians 1:8–11.

d. How have you tested God? What is your antidote to the temptation to manipulate or use God?

4. Close

• Stand, join hands, and recite the Lord's Prayer together.

Fifth Meeting—Week of Five Lent
THE PLACE OF THE OIL PRESS

1. Opening

• Begin with singing and candle lighting.

• [One minute of silence.] *The Christian mystic and Spanish poet St. John of the Cross wrote these verses in one of his poems:

In one dark night,
with longings fired in love,
Oh the sheer grace!
I went out unseen,
my house being now stilled.

In darkness and secure,
by the secret ladder, disguised,
Oh, the sheer grace!
in darkness and in disguise,
my house being now stilled.

In the happy night
in secret, when no one saw me,
nor looked I at anything,
without other light and guide
but the one that burned in my heart.[4]

St. John's phrase "My house being now stilled" speaks to us of the practice of silence in desert spirituality. In referring to this poem, Richard Foster notes: "Every distraction of the body, mind, and spirit must be put into a kind of suspended animation before the deep work of God upon the soul can occur."[5] Take a moment now to still your house, to become centered in silent prayer.

- Say a brief verbal prayer asking for God's continuing presence as we continue our journey into the Lenten Desert.
- If helpful, remind members of their responsibilities to one another and to the group (Appendix B).

2. Gethsemane Prayer Exercise
- Read Matthew 26:36–46.
- Say a prayer asking God's help in entering into Jesus' experience at the oil press, to be able to share in his sorrow, to feel something of his anguish, and to be able to surrender our life as he surrendered his.
- Meditation

a. Ask group members to close their eyes and to relax just as you have been doing.

b. Ask them to do the following: *Imagine that you are in the upper room with Jesus and the disciples. Judas, apparently up to something, has left. Jesus has washed everyone's feet, including yours. The supper is over. Your mind is filled with the strange events and puzzling words of the evening. Slowly you all leave the upper room, make your way down the steps and walk out onto the narrow street. It is late, and the little winding streets are quiet as you make your way to that secret place in the garden.

You approach the entrance to Gethsemane. Is there a gate that you must walk through? Is it a wide or narrow gate? Do you have to walk through one at a time, or can several pass through at once? Whom are you next to? As you walk, how near are you to Jesus? What does it feel like to enter this garden, this ancient and mysterious olive orchard, with Jesus? Imagine in as much detail as you can what your surroundings are like: how dark or light the night, how cool or warm the late night air feels. Pay attention to the little dirt path you are all on. See the olive trees, and smell their fragrance. Can you hear sounds, perhaps the sound of a gentle rustling breeze, or is the night silence? What is the sound you hear or the silence like? Look closely at Jesus. What do you see in his face? What does the way in which Jesus moves and holds his body tell you about his inner feelings and thoughts? You see Jesus go alone over to the old stone oil press. You can see he is praying. You can see his anguish. You begin to ponder the depths of Jesus' love and its obvious connection with his profound sorrow. Reflect for a moment on what it might be like if someone you loved very much were accused and condemned for a serious crime—your friend, your husband, your wife, your mother or father, or perhaps your child. How desperate and helpless would you feel? How agonized would your prayers be? What feelings of shame and hurt would you feel for them and with them? Picture yourself completely alone, deserted or betrayed by everyone who matters to you. See yourself letting go of everything, being emptied of everything, of all hopes, desires or symbols of security, emptied of everything but love. It is the moment of your own death. There is no absolute scientific certitude of what, if anything, lies beyond the door. Can you embrace the moment, can you entrust yourself into God's keeping, can you go on loving no matter what? Now imagine as best as you can the sorrow, the humiliation, the pain of Jesus in embracing the whole world in limitless love, suffering the isolation, the alienation, and the loneliness from those he loved, trusting that to die in love is the only way to live.

In closing, talk with Jesus in your heart. Talk with Christ about how any experience of your own human loving gives you insight into his compassion. Thank Christ for loving you and the entire world with such unreserved, extravagant, self-giving love. Join with Jesus in his simple prayer: "Abba, not my will but yours be done."

When you are ready, open your eyes and rejoin the group.

3. Discussion
- As time permits, you might discuss any or all the following:
a. What came up for you during this exercise?
b. Have you ever felt like the life was being crushed out of you? Were you able to deal with it through surrender?
c. What do you do by way of making spiritual preparation? What is your waiting, watching, and praying like? Do you have a rule? Would you like to share it?

4. Close:
- Stand, join hands around the circle, and recite the Lord's Prayer together.

Sixth Meeting—Holy Week
CRUCIFORM WISDOM

1. Opening

- Begin with singing and candle lighting. (This time you might want to use the Taizé song "Jesus Remember Me," or "In Our Darkest Night," or both.)
- One minute of silence.

  *Henri J. M. Nouwen wrote: "Without solitude it is virtually impossible to live a spiritual life. Solitude begins with a time and place for God, and God alone. If we really believe not only that God exists but that God is actively present in our lives— healing, teaching, and guiding—we need to set aside time and space to give God our undivided attention. Jesus says, 'Go to your private room and when you have shut your door, pray to your Father who is in that secret place'" (Matt. 6:6).[6] So as usual we will take one minute to go into our inner room and pray in silence to our Father who is in that secret place.

- Conclude with a brief verbal prayer welcoming God's presence.
- If helpful, remind members of their responsibilities to one another and to the group (Appendix B).

2. The Way of the Cross

- *Since our chapter this time dealt with the crucifixion, and since this Friday is Good Friday, the day of Christ's death on the cross, it is appropriate at this meeting for us to practice a form of The Way of the Cross.
a. The devotion known as The Way of the Cross has its origins in a custom practiced by pilgrims to Jerusalem. They would offer prayers at a series of places, or stations, in the city that were associated with Christ's suffering and death.
b. Sometimes fourteen stations are used, six of which are based

on inferences from the Gospels or pious legends, and eight based on events actually recorded in the Gospels. We will use only the eight from the Gospels.

c. The custom is for a series of crosses (the early tradition was to use plain wooden crosses) to be placed along a wall in a church or some other convenient place, with prayer and the reading of Scripture at each station.

• Facilitators please note: It may be possible for you to set up eight stations with crosses and pictorial representations of the event for each station, and to physically move from one place to another. If so, you will need to give clear instructions regarding this "walking meditation" at this point. If you are meeting in someone's living room or somewhere that is very limited in space, then you will need to explain that the entire devotion will be done sitting and that all movement will take place in the participants' imaginations. It may be possible for all of the group members to take part in the readings and prayers. In any case assign as many people as possible, well in advance, to read and pray. Make sure you have made copies of this devotion for those who either do not have books or who may forget their books.

First Station
Jesus is condemned to death.

Leader: O Christ, we bless you and we worship you.
All: *Because by your holy cross you have saved the whole world.*
Reader: "It was early in the morning when Jesus was taken from Caiaphas to the building where the Roman governor stayed. . . . Pilate gave orders for Jesus to be beaten with a whip. The soldiers made a crown out of thorn branches and put it on Jesus. Then they put a purple robe on him. They came up to him and said, 'Hey, you king of the Jews!' They also hit him with their

fists. . . . When the chief priests and temple police saw Jesus, they yelled. 'Nail him to a cross! Nail him to a cross!' Pilate told them, 'You take him and nail him to a cross! I don't find him guilty of anything. . . .' Then Pilate wanted to set Jesus free. But the crowd again yelled. 'If you set this man free you are no friend of the Emperor! Anyone who claims to be a king is an enemy of the Emperor. . . .' When Pilate heard this he brought Jesus out. Then he sat down on the judge's bench. . . . It was about noon on the day before Passover, and Pilate said to the crowd, 'Look at your king!' 'Kill him! Kill him!' they yelled. 'Nail him to a cross!!!!' Then Pilate handed him over to be nailed to a cross" (John 18:28–19:16 CEV).

Leader: God did not spare his own Son:

All: *But delivered him up for us all.*

Leader: Let us pray (silence).

God of Wisdom and Might, as we contemplate the cross we pray that you will bring us to enlightenment. May we grasp the height and depth and breadth of the love you have lavished upon us in Christ Jesus; more than that, we pray that we will be *grasped by* your great eternal love revealed to us in the crucifixion of Jesus Christ, your Son. Amen.

All: *Loving God*
Holy and Mighty One
Have mercy on us.

Second Station
Jesus takes up his Cross.

Leader: O Christ, we bless you and we worship you.

All: *Because by your holy cross you have saved the whole world.*

Reader: "When the soldiers had finished making fun of Jesus, they took off the purple robe. They put his own clothes back on him,

112

and led him off to be nailed to a cross" (Mark 15:20 CEV). "Christ, although He existed in the form of God, did not regard equality with God a thing to be grasped, but emptied Himself, taking the form of a bondservant, and being made in the likeness of men. And being found in appearance as a man, He humbled Himself by becoming obedient to the point of death, even death on a cross" (Philippians 2:6–8).

Leader: Surely he has borne our grief:

All: *And carried our sorrows.*

Leader: Let us pray (silence).

God of Love, we see now that in yielding to the cross Christ was yielding to the way of Love. That in yielding completely to your will Jesus was choosing to be guided by Love. We understand more and more clearly how the cross was an offering of pure love. Amen.

All: *Loving God*

Holy and Mighty One Have mercy on us.

Third Station
The Cross is laid on Simon of Cyrene.

Leader: O Christ, we bless you and we worship you.

All: *Because by your holy cross you have saved the whole world.*

Reader: "When the soldiers had finished making fun of Jesus, they took off the robe. They put his own clothes back on him and led him off to be nailed to a cross. On the way they met a man from Cyrene named Simon, and they forced him to carry Jesus' cross" (Matthew 27:31, 32 CEV). "If anyone would come after me, let him deny himself and take up his cross and follow me" (Matthew 16:24). "He who seeks only his illusory false self brings his true self to ruin: whereas he who brings his false self to naught for me discovers who he is—i.e. the image of God,

his true self" (Matthew 10:38-39, paraphrase by Thelma Hall).[7]
Leader: Whoever does not bear his own cross and come after me:
All: *Cannot be my disciple.*
Leader: Let us pray (silence).

Gracious God, by the compassion of Christ you have set us free. You have liberated us not by removing all suffering from our world or from us, but by sharing it fully with us. Make us, then, partners in the suffering of Christ—that suffering in which joy and strength are perfected. Give us the courage and faith to take up our own cross and follow Christ in the way of unrestrained compassion and self-giving love. Amen.

All: *Loving God*
Holy and Mighty One Have mercy on us

Fourth Station
Jesus meets the women of Jerusalem on the Via Dolorosa.

Leader: O Christ, we bless you and we worship you.
All: *Because by your holy cross you have saved the whole world.*
Reader: "A large crowd was following Jesus, and in the crowd a lot of women were crying and weeping for him. Jesus turned to the women and said: 'Women of Jerusalem, don't cry for me! Cry for yourselves and your children'" (Luke 23:27-28 CEV). "Our God, you bless everyone whose sins you forgive and wipe away. You bless them by saying, 'You told me your sins, without trying to hide them, and now I forgive you.' You are my hiding place! You protect me from trouble, and put songs in my heart because you have saved me" (Psalm 32:1-2, 7 CEV).
Leader: Those who have sown in tears:
All: *Shall reap with songs of joy.*
Leader: Let us pray (silence).

O God, you are to us "silent music." Your presence is sweeter than life. Christ is the song in our heart. In the crucifixion of Christ we have found forgiveness and new life. We believe your promise that in unwavering faith true joy will well up from the core of our being. Amen.

All: *Loving God*
Holy and Mighty One Have mercy on us.

Fifth Station
Jesus is stripped of his clothes.

Leader: O Christ, we bless you and we worship you.

All: *Because by your holy cross you have saved the whole world.*

Reader: "The soldiers took Jesus to Golgotha, which means 'Place of the Skull.' There they gave him some wine mixed with a drug to ease the pain, but he refused to drink it. . . . They divided up his clothes into four parts, one for each of them. But his outer garment was made from a single piece of cloth, and it did not have any seams. The soldiers said to each other, 'Let's not rip it apart. We will gamble to see who gets it.' This happened so that the Scriptures would come true, which say, 'They divided up my clothes and gambled for my garments.' The soldiers then did what they had decided" (Mark 15:22; John 19:23–25 CEV).

Leader: They gave me gall to eat:

All: *And when I was thirsty they gave me vinegar to drink.*

Leader: Let us pray (silence).

Almighty God, in the stripping of Christ, in the naked poverty of Christ, we see your unimaginable humility. We are utterly astounded by the self-emptying love of Christ. With fear and trembling we pray that we may follow this same way of abandoning everything for your love. Amen.

All: *Loving God*
Holy and Mighty One Have mercy on us.

Sixth Station
Jesus is nailed to the Cross.

Leader: O Christ, we bless you and we worship you.

All: *Because by your holy cross you have saved the whole world.*

Reader: "They nailed Jesus to the cross. . . . It was about nine o'-clock in the morning when they nailed him to the cross. On it was a sign that told why he was nailed there. It read, 'This is the King of the Jews.' The soldiers also nailed two criminals on crosses, one to the right of Jesus and the other to his left. People who passed by said terrible things about Jesus. They shook their heads and shouted, 'Ha! So you're the one who claimed you could tear down the temple and build it again in three days. Save yourself and come down from the cross!' The chief priests and the teachers of the Law of Moses also made fun of Jesus. They said to each other, 'He saved others but he can't save himself. If he is the Messiah, the king of Israel, let him come down from the cross! Then we will see and believe.' The two criminals also said cruel things to Jesus" (Mark 15:24–32 CEV).

Leader: They pierce my hands and feet:

All: *They stare and gloat over me.*

Leader: Let us pray (silence).

Gracious Father, what a wonder you are. You love us, you guide us, you live inside us. You have given us your Son that we might be fully and wonderfully alive. Help us to accept fully your love which makes everything else possible. We know Father that it was not the iron spikes that held Jesus to the cross, but his limitless love for you and for the whole world. May we also be nailed to the cross of Christ by this same love for you and for one another. Amen.

All: *Loving God*
Holy and Mighty One
Have mercy on us.

116

Seventh Station
Jesus dies on the Cross.

Leader: O Christ, we bless you and we worship you.

All: *Because by your holy cross you have saved the whole world.*

Reader: "Around noon the sky turned dark and stayed that way until the middle of the afternoon. The sun stopped shining, and the curtain in the temple split down the middle. Jesus shouted, 'Father, I put myself in your hands.' Then he died. A crowd had gathered to see the terrible sight. Then after they had seen it, they felt brokenhearted and went home. All of Jesus' close friends and the women who had come with him from Galilee stood at a distance and watched" (Luke 23:44–49 CEV).

Leader: Let us pray (silence).

Lord, before the mystery of the crucifixion we are filled with reverence, with awe. In the darkness of the crucifixion is our light. In the weakness of the cross is our power. In the absurdity of Jesus' death is our wisdom. In the tearing of the curtain is our entrance into Holy Communion with you. Teach us, O Lord, to know nothing but Christ crucified. Amen.

All: *Loving God*
Holy and Mighty One
Have mercy on us.

Station Eight
Jesus is laid in the tomb.

Leader: O Christ, we bless you and we worship you.

All: *Because by your holy cross you have saved the whole world.*

Reader: "That evening a rich disciple named Joseph from the town of Arimathea went and asked for Jesus' body. Pilate gave orders for it to be given to Joseph, who took the body and wrapped it in a clean linen cloth. Then Joseph put the body in his own tomb that had never been used. He rolled a big stone against the entrance to the tomb and went away. All this time Mary Magdalene and the other Mary were sitting across from the tomb" (Matthew 27:57–61 CEV).

Leader: Let us pray (silence)

Father, may the life of Jesus Christ, your Son, flow into us as the life of the vine flows into the branches. May Christ's body and blood be our food and our drink. May his passion and death be wisdom and strength in our heart. We thank you, O Christ, for your great love and ask that you disclose to us more of the mystery of your death—the death that gives life.

All: *Loving God*

Holy and Mighty One

Have Mercy on us.

(Allow for a brief silence before moving on.)

3. Discussion

- If time permits you might discuss the following:
a. Were you able, in this exercise, to experience anything of Jesus' self-giving love?
b. Have you come to any new insights, or have you been reminded of an old insight into the meaning of the cross?
c. What does it mean to you to empty yourself until only love for God and others is left?
d. Do you have any comments or observations, or questions you would like to raise regarding this chapter?

4. Close

- Stand and say the Lord's Prayer together.

Seventh Meeting—Easter Week
A VISION OF THE MOON

1. Opening
- Begin with singing and candle lighting.
- Read Luke 24:13–35 from *The Message* or some other contemporary version.
- Say a verbal prayer welcoming Christ's presence as the risen Lord.
- Remind members of their responsibilities to one another and to the group (Appendix B).

2. Centering or Contemplative Prayer
- Instructions/script
a. *This time we are going to practice ten minutes of centering prayer, and then we will use the remainder of our time for discussion. In this kind of prayer we truly enter the desert stillness. In centering prayer we are instructed by the words of Psalm 46:10, "Be still and know that I am God." In centering prayer we do not use words, or pictures, or thoughts. A thought is anything of which you become conscious. Of course, we can't make our minds go completely blank, but we don't have to grab hold of our thoughts. Think of your consciousness as being like a river. All sorts of things come floating down the river—logs, rafts, boats of all shapes and sizes and colors. You can't keep them from floating down the river, but you can just let them float by without paying them any great attention. Let everything go and sit quietly in the presence of God. Many people find it helpful to repeat a "sacred word" whenever they are distracted—Abba, Lord, love, faith, or some other word from Scripture. Repeating the sacred word helps them not to become entangled with the thought and to return to their intention to be with God in silence.

So, settle into a comfortable position with your feet flat on the floor, your back straight, and your eyes closed. Take a deep breath and hold it to the count of four. Exhale slowly like a big sigh. [Repeat three times.] Scan your body from head to toe and relax any areas of tension. Allow your breath to become deep, slow, and regular. Deep, slow, and regular. Let all distractions float away. Spiral down into the deepest place within you where Christ dwells. You might imagine yourself descending to great depths in an elevator, or going down flights of stairs, going down, descending deeper and deeper. Or imagine that you are descending into a bottomless pool of water, going deeper and deeper. Don't try to make anything happen. Don't try to prevent anything from happening. Simply be in God's loving presence. Let everything go.

b. Ten minutes of silence.

c. *Take a little time to come out of the silence. When you are ready, open your eyes and rejoin the group.

• You may discuss what the silence was like for people or anything that emerged out of the silence for anyone.

3. Discussion

• You may want to use the following discussion questions for the remainder of your time.

1. During this "desert time'" what have you learned about God? How has God seemed to you during this time?

2. What have you learned about yourself?

3. What do you desire for the future in terms of your relationship with God?

4. Where do you want to go from here in terms of your spiritual practice?

5. As we conclude these times together, what are you feeling?

4. Close

- Explain that what is important is that we have been in the desert. That what matters more than any experience we may have had is the purity of our intention to be with God. If we can keep returning to that intention, powerful things will happen in our inner life.

- Ask someone to read the following excerpt from one of Henri Nouwen's Easter meditations:

  Easter season is a time of hope. There still is fear, there still is a painful awareness of sinfulness, but there is light breaking though. Something new is happening, something that goes beyond the changing moods of our life. We can be joyful or sad, optimistic or pessimistic, tranquil or angry, but the stream of God's presence moves deeper than the small waves of our minds and hearts. Easter brings the awareness that God is present even when his presence is not directly noticed. Easter brings the good news that, although things seem to get worse in the world, the Evil One has already been overcome. Easter allows us to affirm that although God seems very distant and although we remain preoccupied with many little things, our Lord walks with us on the road and keeps explaining the Scripture to us. Thus there are many rays of hope casting their light on our way through life.[8]

  Stand in a circle, join hands, and repeat the Lord's Payer together.

References

Introduction
1. Thomas Merton, *What Is Contemplation?* (Springfield, Ill.: Templegate Publishers, 1950), 7.

I. Into the Desert
Epigraph: Edward Abbey, *Desert Solitaire: A Season in the Wilderness* (New York: Simon and Schuster, 1968), 132.
1. Hosea 2:14–15.
2. Matthew 16:25 (*The Message*).
3. Gerald E. May, *The Awakened Heart: Living beyond Addiction* (San Francisco: Harper and Collins Publishers, 1991), 2.
4. *The Sayings and Stories of the Christian Fathers of Egypt: The Paradise of the Fathers*, English trans. of *Apothegmata Patrum* by E. A. Wallis Budge (London: Kegan Paul, 2002), 14.
5. Thomas Merton, *The Wisdom of the Desert: Sayings from the Desert Fathers of the Fourth Century* (New York: New Directions Books, 1960), 3.
6. Ephesians 6:12.
7. John 18:38.
8. Barbara Brown Taylor, "Physics and Faith: The Luminous Web," *Christian Century*, 116, 17 (June 2–9, 1999): 612–19.

II. Alleluia is the Song
Epigraph: Thomas Merton, *Contemplative Prayer* (Garden City, N.Y.: Doubleday and Company, 1971), 27.
1. Mark 1:12 (NIV).
2. Thomas Merton, *Life and Holiness* (Garden City, N. Y.: Doubleday and Company, 1963), 59.
3. John 3:16.
4. C. S. Lewis, *Mere Christianity* (New York: Macmillan Company,

1960), 138–39.

5. Ibid., 139.

6. Ephesians 4:6 (NRSV).

7. Lewis, *Mere Christianity,* 156.

8. Matthew 3:16–17 *(The Message).*

9. John 1:1–5 (NRSV).

10. Lao Tsu, *Tao Te Ching,* trans. Gia-Fu Feng and Jane English (New York: Random House Publishers, 1972), 1, 4, 16, 25, 41, 51.

11. John 14:6 (NRSV).

12. John 6:53 (NRSV).

13. Luke 9:10,12.

14. John 6:49–52 (NRSV).

15. John 6:51 (NRSV).

16. John 6:27 (NRSV).

17. Merton, *Contemplative Prayer,* 27.

III. The Conjurer

Epigraph: *Rabbi Nachman's Wisdom,* trans. Aryeh Kaplan (New York: Breslov Research Institute, 1984), 111–12.

1. Rollo May, *Power and Innocence: A Search for the Source of Violence* (New York: W. W. Norton Company, 1972), 121.

2. Matthew 22:37–39.

3. Charles T. Tart, *Living the Mindful Life: A Handbook for Living in the Present Moment* (Boston: Shambhala, 1994), 16, 17.

4. Ibid., 18.

5. William Blake, "Eternity," in *The Oxford Book of Nineteenth Century English Verse* (Oxford: Oxford University Press, 1964), 26.

6. John 8:44–45 (NRSV).

7. W. H. Auden, "The Witnesses," in *The Collected Poetry of W. H. Auden* (New York: Random House ,1945), 185.

8. D. Elton Trueblood, *The Essence of Spiritual Religion* (New York: Harper and Row Publishers, 1936), 10.

IV. The Third Test

Epigraph: René Voillaume, *Brothers of Men: Letters to the Petits Frères,* ed. Lancelot Sheppard (Baltimore: Helicone Press, 1966), 97–98.

1. Exodus 17:3.

2. Exodus 17:7 (NRSV).

3. Deuteronomy 6:16 (NRSV).

4. Robert Johnson, *He: Understanding Masculine Psychology,* rev. ed. (New York: Harper and Row, 1989), 6, 7.

5. Gerald G. May, *Will and Spirit: A Contemplative Psychology* (San Francisco: Harper and Row, 1982), 53.
6. Galatians 2:20 (NRSV).
7. Dietrich Bonhoeffer, *The Cost of Discipleship* (New York: Macmillan Company, 1959), "Who Am I?" 15.
8. Thomas Keating, *The Mystery of Christ: The Liturgy as Spiritual Experience* (New York: Continuum Publishing Company, 1997), 41, 42.
9. Wayne E. Oates, *When Religion Gets Sick* (Philadelphia: Westminster Press, 1970), 52.

V. The Place of the Oil Press
Epigraph: James Finley, *Merton's Palace of Nowhere: A Search for God through Awareness of the True Self* (Notre Dame, Ind.: Ave Maria Press, 1978), 13.
1. Henri J. M. Nouwen, *Can You Drink the Cup?* (Notre Dame, Ind.: Ave Maria Press, 1996).
2. J. B. Phillips, *Your God Is Too Small* (New York: Macmillan Publishing Company, 1961), 75.
3. Dallas Willard, *The Spirit of the Disciplines* (San Francisco: Harper and Row Publishers, 1988), 6.
4. M. Scott Peck, *The Road Less Traveled* (New York: Simon and Schuster, 1978), 77.
5. T. S. Eliot, "East Coker," in *Four Quartets: The Centenary Edition* (San Diego: Harcourt Brace Jovanovich Publishers, 1943, 1971), 29.
6. Romans 8:24–25 (NIV).
7. Nan C. Merrill, *Psalms for Praying* (New York: Continuum, 1996), 119.
8. Matthew 26:40–41 *(The Message)*.
9. William Wordsworth, "Lines Composed a Few Miles above Tintern Abbey," in *The Oxford Book of Nineteenth Century English Verse* (Oxford: Oxford University Press, 1964), 69.
10. Lao Tsu, *Tao Te Ching*, trans. Gia-Fu Feng and Jane English, (New York: Random House Publishers, 1972), 15.

VI. Cruciform Wisdom
Epigraph: Barbara Brown Taylor, *God in Pain: Teaching Sermons on Suffering* (Nashville: Abingdon Press, 1998), 105.
1. Edward Abbey, *Desert Solitaire: A Season in the Wilderness* (New York: Simon and Schuster, 1968), 5, 6.
2. 1 Corinthians 1:18 *(The Message)*.
3. 1 Corinthians 1:19–20; 2:6–8 *(The Message)*.

4. Hans Conzelmann, *A Commentary on the First Epistle to the Corinthians,* trans. James W. Leitch (Philadelphia: Fortress Press, 1975), 49, 50.
5. Norman Mailer, *The Naked and the Dead* (New York: Henry Holt Company, 1998), 323.
6. Quoted in Robert Herbert Albers, *The Theological and Psychological Dynamics of Transformation in the Recovery from the Disease of Alcoholism* (Ann Arbor, Mich.: University Microfilms International, 1982; authorized facsimile, 1983), 92.
7. Ibid.
8. James 3:17 (NRSV).
9. William Johnston, *Lord Teach Us to Pray: Christian Zen and the Inner Eye of Love* (London: Harper Collins, 1990), 296–98.
10. Stephen Hawking, *A Brief History of Time: From the Big Bang to Black Holes* (New York: Bantam Books, 1988), 175.
11. 1 Corinthians 2:16 (CEV).

VII.A Vision of the Moon
Epigraph: William Johnston, *Lord Teach Us to Pray: Christian Zen and the Inner Eye of Love* (London: Harper Collins Publishers, 1991), 64.
1. Rollo May, *My Quest For Beauty* (San Francisco: Saybrook Publishing Company, 1985), 59–60.
2. Isaiah 40:6.
3. T. S. Eliot, "East Coker," in *Four Quartets: The Centenary Edition* (San Diego: Harcourt Brace Jovanovich Publishers, 1943, 1971), 28.
4. Luke 24:25 (NRSV).
5. Thomas Merton, *He Is Risen* (Niles, Ill.: Argus Communications, 1975), 46–51.
6. Johnston, *Lord Teach Us To Pray,* 66.
7. Luke 24:27 (NRSV).
8. John 5:39–40 (NIV).
9. Watchman Nee, *What Shall This Man Do?* (Fort Washington, Pa.: Christian Literature Crusade, 1961, 1973), 116.
10. Luke 24:32 (NRSV).
11. Henri J. M. Nouwen, *With Burning Hearts: A Meditation on the Eucharistic Life* (Maryknoll, N.Y.: Orbis Books, 1994), 57.
12. Ibid., 65, 68.
13. Luke 24:30–31 (CEV).
14. Nouwen, *With Burning Hearts,* 68–69
15. John Polkinghorne, *Quarks, Chaos, and Christianity: Questions to Science and Religion* (New York: Crossroad Publishers, 1996), 92, 93.

16. Charles Perry, *The Resurrection Promise: An Interpretation of the Easter Narrative* (Grand Rapids, Mich.: W. B. Eerdmans, 1986), 7, 8.
17. C. W. McPherson, *Understanding Faith: An Exploration of Christian Theology* (Harrisburg, Pa.: Morehouse Publishing, 1998), 118.
18. Gerald O'Collins. S.J., *What Are They Saying about the Resurrection?* (New York: Paulist Press, 1978), 41–67.
19. Gerald O'Collins, S.J., *The Resurrection of Jesus Christ* (Milwaukee: Judson Press, 1973), 32, 33.
20. John 1:14 (NRSV).
21. Colossians 1:17 (NIV).
22. John 14:6; 15:1 (NRSV).
23. John 12:32 (NRSV).

Appendix A. About Small Groups

1. Norvene Vest, *Gathered in the Word: Praying the Scripture in Small Groups* (Nashville: Upper Room Books, 1996).
2. Jacqueline Syrup Bergan and S. Marie Schwan, *Surrender: A Guide to Prayer* (Winona, Minn.: Saint Mary's Press, 1986).
3. Thelma Hall, RC, *Too Deep for Words: Rediscovering Lectio Divina* (New York: Paulist Press, 1988).
4. Rose Mary Dougherty, *Group Spiritual Direction: Community for Discernment* (New York: Paulist Press, 1995), 94.
5. Ibid., 13.
6. Ibid., 13.

Appendix C. Spiritual Exercises for Small Groups

1. Gerald May, *The Awakened Heart: Living beyond Addiction* (San Francisco: Harper Collins Publishers, 1991), 1–3.
2. Frederick W. Faber, "To Breathe the Name."
3. Henri J. M. Nouwen, *The Way of the Heart: Desert Spirituality and Contemporary Ministry* (Minneapolis: Seabury Press, 1981), 43, 69.
4. St. John of the Cross, "Noche Oscura," in *Saint John of the Cross: From Anabaptist Spirituality*, trans. Hugo Zorrilla trans. (Fresno, Calif., 1993), 67.
5. Richard Foster, *Prayer: Finding the Heart's True Home* (San Francisco: Harper Collins Publishers, 1992), 163.
6. Nouwen, *The Way of the Heart*, 30, 31.
7. Thelma Hall, *Too Deep for Words: Rediscovering Lectio Divina* (New York: Paulist Press, 1988), 24.
8. Henri J. M. Nouwen, *Show Me the Way: Readings for Each Day of Lent* (New York: Crossroad Publishing, 1992), 139, 140.